Preschool
Preparedness
for an
Emergency

ANDREW ROSZAK,
JD, MPA, EMT-PARAMEDIC

Dedication

Dedicated to those professionals who get up every day and selflessly provide their care and compassion to help educate our children.

Table of Contents

Acknowledgments

This is the second book in the Preparing for the Unexpected series. During the course of writing this book, Mother Nature again reinforced the value of this series. Beginning in December 2019, Puerto Rico began to experience a series of earthquakes. These tremors (*terremotos* in Spanish) continued to plague the island for more than a month. In January 2020, I was with our team in Puerto Rico working with early childhood programs. In one week alone, there were more than 487 earthquakes. The situation was dire, with many people sleeping outside in tents out of fear that the next quake would cause their homes to collapse.

Neighborhoods banded together and developed tent cities that served as little communities. In these tent cities, people shared resources, swapped stories, and found compassion. Not surprisingly, many of the tent communities formed near or even on property used for early childhood programming. In Guánica, for example, families sought shelter in tents directly behind the playground used for Head Start. In Peñuelas, a tent city arose next to the Head Start building. The images paint a picture worth reflecting on, and one I hope this book helps to underscore: *early childhood education is a vital component of the community.*

While the weeks and tremors came and went, early childhood professionals rose to the task. Teachers could no longer teach in their programs, as many buildings were damaged and shut down for safety reasons or condemned. Instead of sitting idle, these extraordinary individuals packed up their teaching supplies and began providing services to the children living in the tent communities. Others took it upon themselves to go out and visit children at their homes— taking time to ensure the family was well fed and stocked with supplies.

Their dedication allowed for a small sense of normalcy to return. Children were able to continue learning, and families gladly welcomed familiar faces. It is hard to put into words, but hopefully this story illustrates to some small degree the passion, dedication, and importance of the early childhood workforce. The following pages are dedicated to those professionals who get up every day and selflessly provide their care and compassion to help educate our children. I hope the contents of this publication provide you with the tools, resources, and knowledge you need to make your program more prepared and resilient.

There are many individuals who have helped with the writing of this publication. Many thanks to Ronald Roszak, Joan Roszak, Amy Roszak, Ruth Roszak, Robert Plechaty, Joyce Plechaty, Maria Rubin, Marty Rubin, Dr. Kathy Morgan, Carole Rubin, and Evan Rubin. I'm so grateful for the support, encouragement, and love of these individuals. A special thanks to my wife, Dr. Sara Roszak, who continues to inspire and amaze me on a daily basis.

A special thanks to Josely A. Bravo González, Jessica Irizarry-Ramos, Jeffrey Droz, and the many other dedicated professionals at the Puerto Rico Department of Health for their work in supporting the children and families in Puerto Rico. Likewise, I greatly respect and appreciate Director Edwin Curbelo Rodríguez's lifelong dedication and passion on these issues.

Further, I greatly appreciate all the efforts by the Institute for Childhood Preparedness staff, who work every day to keep children safe. The efforts of Elisa Greenberg, Amy Lowery, Emily Adams, and Nikki Fernandes are beyond deserving of special thanks. It is an inspiration to work with such wonderful individuals. Finally, many thanks to Iran Rodriguez, Dr. David Dyjack, and Yvette Sanchez-Fuentes. It is an honor to work alongside you, and I am in deep gratitude for your continued willingness to share your wisdom and guidance.

Childhood Preparedness at a Glance

Caring for children is not an easy task. Every day in the United States, an estimated two million early childhood professionals care for approximately ten million children under the age of five, according to the *Early Childhood Workforce Index 2018* (Whitebook et al., 2018). In addition, the National Center for Education Statistics (2019) states that 56.6 million students attended elementary, middle, and high schools during fall 2019. Children under the age of eighteen make up nearly 25 percent of the US population, and each day approximately seventy million children spend the majority of their waking hours away from their families in child care, school, or after-school programs.

While much attention and many resources have been developed to assist principals and administrators serving K–12 educational institutions in emergency preparedness, relatively few resources exist to aid early childhood professionals. The lack of available resources on this topic for early childhood programs is one of the many reasons for this publication.

The simple fact is that early childhood education is of paramount importance. Children spend vastly more time at early childhood programs than they do in programs that serve older children. In comparison to the hours spent in K–12 settings, children spend ten times more hours in early childhood programs. During their most formative years, millions of children under the age of five spend thousands of hours per year in a paid child-care setting (Stevens, 2017).

Early childhood programs include infants who are entirely dependent on others to toddlers who can engage in activities and learning. Prekindergarten is the next step in children's lives, setting them up for a classroom environment in kindergarten. The impact on a child's development largely comes from early childhood learning environments (Stevens, 2017).

On average, children spend about thirty-six hours a week in child care. This reality places a tremendous responsibility on early childhood professionals, especially since the occurrence of disasters is on the rise. From 2016 to 2018, on average there were fifteen disasters each year that were billion-dollar crises. In comparison, from 1980 to 2018 the average was just 6.2 events per year (Eschner, 2019; Federal Emergency Management Agency [FEMA], 2019). In addition to ensuring that children have a nurturing and educational environment, we must also ensure that we are providing a safe environment.

The challenges of providing a safe environment are compounded by children's unique physical, emotional, and developmental needs, such as need for routine, reliance on adults, opportunity to expend energy by playing outdoors, and emergence of self-awareness and awareness of emotion-eliciting events. Because of these needs, the US Department of Health and Human Services (HHS) classifies children as an at-risk population. Simply put, we must be prepared to protect those who are unable to prepare and protect themselves.

Changing societal norms have also increased the prominence and importance of the early childhood workforce. Around forty years ago, less than half of all mothers worked outside of the home, and only a third of mothers with a child under age three worked outside of the home. In contrast, 65.1 percent of mothers with children under the age of six were in the labor force in 2018 (US Department of Labor, Bureau of Labor Statistics, 2020).

Even with these shifting demographics and roles of parents, a recent study found that 35 percent of households in the United States were not familiar with their school's evacuation and emergency plans, and 41 percent were unaware where their children would be evacuated to in the case of a disaster (Schlegelmilch, 2018). Sadly, early childhood is not immune to emergencies and disasters, and we have also struggled to articulate the importance of preparing for disasters for our most vulnerable children aged birth to five years. Further, federal funding to support emergency preparedness and improving children's safety has lagged far behind. An examination of federal preparedness funding from 2004–2012 revealed that federal emergency-preparedness grants that support children's safety equal less than one cent of every ten dollars invested (Save the Children, 2015).

There is a clear need to ensure early childhood programs are prepared for emergencies. But, after every disaster, we see systemic failures that point to the need to further improve policies and procedures for children. These failures occur partly because of our misconceptions around the abilities, capabilities, and limitations of emergency responders. As we have become more reliant on technology and on-demand services, our expectations have changed. A recent study revealed that 51 percent of Americans believe that, during a disaster, help will arrive in less than sixty minutes (Petkova et al., 2016). This finding highlights the disconnect between expectations and reality during a disaster. Contrary to public perception, during a disaster or large-scale emergency, help will not be available for a prolonged time— likely measured in hours, not minutes.

This reality underscores the importance of emergency-preparedness planning for early childhood programs. These plans are necessary because we are very likely to be on our own during the initial stages of a disaster. It is incumbent on us to prepare for these types of situations, and that means ensuring we are self-sufficient for up to seventy-two hours. Preplanning

It is incumbent on us to prepare for emergency situations, and that means ensuring we are self-sufficient for up to seventy-two hours.

allows us to think through these issues. Purchasing food, water, and supplies is a wise investment and one that may prove extremely useful in a disaster.

Some recent examples highlight the impact disasters can have on the child-care sector:

- In October 2010, Superstorm Sandy caused the long-term closure of 697 child-care programs in Connecticut, New Jersey, and New York. Some programs were closed for up to eight months before reopening. Many of the programs suffered financial hardships beyond just the physical damages. When reopening, some early childhood programs found that the children they served before the storm did not return; they had either moved away or sought care elsewhere (Murrin, 2015).

- The Louisiana flooding in 2016 impacted at least eighty-eight child-care programs in the Baton Rouge area, displacing more than 6,000 children from their child-care programs. A month later, forty-five programs remained closed (Roszak, 2017).

- During Hurricane Matthew in 2016, more than a quarter of the child-care providers in Cumberland County, North Carolina, closed, leaving an estimated 10,200 children temporarily without child care (Roszak, 2017).

- In October 2018, Hurricane Michael interrupted 417 early childhood programs in Georgia. These programs cared for an estimated 16,680 children. More than three hundred programs closed for at least one day. Loss of water and/or power was cited as the number one reason for the closure (Institute for Childhood Preparedness, 2019a).

- In 2020, nearly half of child-care centers shut down because of the COVID-19 pandemic. Of the facilities that remained open, 85 percent operated at less than 50 percent enrollment capacity, with many operating at less than 25 percent capacity (Guynn, 2020).

All of these disasters impacted the child-care providers and also exacted a tremendous toll on children, families, employers, and the communities at large.

Throughout the following pages, you will find information designed to help increase your emergency-preparedness knowledge. Real-world events and case studies will provide a backdrop to help further explore and understand these issues. The ultimate goal is to provide you with the knowledge and the resources needed to ensure that your early childhood program is prepared.

Defining Emergency Preparedness

Emergency preparedness is an ongoing cycle of cycle of mitigation, preparation, and recovery.

(FEMA, 2013)

Mitigation efforts seek to reduce potential harm or loss from emergencies or disasters. Mitigation activities are done in advance and involve conducting activities to lower risk. For example, a city may enact building codes to reduce the effects of high winds or floods on buildings. By enacting these codes, the city is seeking to reduce the potential losses that may be incurred from a disaster. Another example of mitigation is purchasing insurance. Insurance may not reduce losses, but it will help a facility bounce back more quickly when an emergency occurs.

Preparation involves the development and testing of emergency action plans. Preparedness is a continuing commitment, which requires monetary investment. Organizations should not view preparedness as complete once the plan is written. Instead, they should test the plan and then reevaluate whether or not the plan is sufficient or needs revisions. Other examples of preparedness include stockpiling food and water.

Response occurs when an emergency or disaster begins. It requires us to take action to protect lives and property. During a response, our investments in planning and training are put to the test. This is game day; this is go time. Organizations that have invested in their mitigation and preparedness efforts will have responses that are effective and efficient. This limits damage and loss of life and allows us to move past the emergency in a more expeditious manner.

Recovery occurs after the immediate threat to life and property has ended. Recovery involves picking up the pieces and attempting to return to normal. Recovery can be a long road; for some communities, it may take years to fully recover. Recovery often involves both short- and long-term efforts. For example, establishing a shelter to meet the needs of displaced individuals is a short-term recovery goal. A long-term recovery goal would be rebuilding homes destroyed by the disaster. Each recovery effort seeks to bring stability to the impacted community (FEMA, 2011).

Mitigation, preparation, response, and recovery work together to help increase preparedness and limit loss. Through incorporating these principles we can seek to:

- limit the amount of time our businesses are closed.
- reduce financial impacts through purchasing insurance.
- reduce the likelihood that we are impacted by making changes to our buildings.
- develop systems that allow us to respond quickly.
- increase staff self-confidence by ensuring everyone understands our plans and is empowered to act.
- satisfy licensing and other regulatory requirements.
- make the families we serve more prepared and convey our commitment to safety.
- develop meaningful relationships with local emergency-response organizations to ensure they recognize the vital role we play in the community's economy.

2 Understanding the Necessity of Preparedness in Child Care

No one ever expects or wants to be in a disaster. Yet we must recognize that disasters and emergencies occur daily in the United States. They occur without regard to age, location, socioeconomic status, or time of day. Anyone anywhere, at anytime could be impacted. According to FEMA data, there were 101 declared disasters in 2019 alone (FEMA, 2019). Many smaller or localized disasters do not rise to the level of a federally declared disaster, so the true number of disasters is much higher.

The number of costly disasters is on the rise. This is for a variety of reasons: increased population and density, increased economic activity, and changes in climate. The past five years have seen ten or more billion-dollar weather disasters in the United States, including fourteen weather disasters that cost more than one billion dollars each in 2019 (National Oceanic and Atmospheric Administration [NOAA], National Centers for Environmental Information [NCEI], 2020).

When examining the disasters that have impacted the United States since 1980, severe storms are by far the most frequent. Since 1980, there have been 241 disasters that have cost more than a billion dollars (Smith, 2019). Of these, 103 or 42.7 percent have been severe storms. The next closest disaster type is tropical cyclones, which occurred forty-two times.

Being prepared is not just creating a plan. Being prepared is a mindset, a lifestyle. It does not mean being paranoid or living in a constant state of fear; rather, it means understanding the risks present in our everyday lives. Once we better understand these risks, we can then take steps to reduce the likelihood or the impact of these risks.

Consider the risks of a fire within your facility. From 2011–2015, fire departments responded to 4,980 fires in educational properties, an approximate average of one thousand fires a year (Campbell, 2017). These included fires at child-care centers; nurseries; elementary, junior, and high schools; and college classroom buildings. These fires caused an average of one death as well as seventy injuries each year. They were also responsible for seventy million dollars in property damage (Campbell, 2017).

Fires at child-care centers average about 560 per year, or more than one a day. Nearly 70 percent of these fires involved cooking equipment. Almost half (48 percent) of fires in child-care centers occurred between 6 a.m. and noon (Campbell, 2017). By practicing proven fire-safety and prevention techniques, we can implement policies and procedures that will lower our risk of fire. For example, good housekeeping reduces the amount of debris and clutter in the building, thus reducing our overall fire load and minimizing the number of contents that are available to catch fire and burn. This preventive step helps reduce the potential severity of a fire and, therefore, lowers risk. Similarly, ensuring smoke detectors, fire-suppression systems, and fire extinguishers are in good working order also limits our risk.

Early childhood professionals serve a unique population—children! Our clientele has limited mobility, often the inability to communicate with words, and a lack of comprehension and perceived risk of danger. These are just a few of the characteristics of the children we serve. When compared to the majority of other workplaces, we have some unique day-to-day challenges, and these are further compounded during emergencies or disasters.

Emergency-Preparedness Requirements

Recognizing the unique environment that early childhood providers function in, regulatory agencies have imposed a series of emergency-preparedness requirements. These are not meant to be punitive but rather are meant to protect the children in our care. These requirements can come from local, state, or federal governments. Further, some funding sources also mandate specific requirements around emergency preparedness.

Child Care and Development Fund Requirements

The reauthorization of the Child Care and Development Block Grant (CCDBG) Act in November 2014 made important updates to how the Child Care and Development Fund (CCDF) is administered. These changes have had profound effects, as CCDF serves 1.4 million children each month and provides funding to nearly 340,000 child-care providers each year (Office of Child Care, 2017).

Under the new requirements, lead agencies must develop and maintain comprehensive plans to address emergency preparedness, response, and recovery efforts for child care. This includes demonstrating how the lead agencies will address the needs of children before, during, and after a state of emergency or major disaster. To fulfill these requirements, lead agencies are required to establish formal connections with key emergency preparedness stakeholders, such as the state emergency management authority, local child-care resource and referral agencies, and public health departments (CCDF, 2019). Further, the disaster plan must also address how child-care services and subsidy payments will continue during emergencies and disasters. This requirement is designed to ensure families will continue to receive both child-care and subsidy benefits in times of crisis. This continuation of care may be at an existing location, an emergency shelter, or even at an alternative site.

The availability of child care in a post-disaster setting is vital for families, as it allows adults time and space to begin to take the steps necessary to begin recovery. Conditions following an emergency or disaster are not likely to be ideal. Therefore, lead agencies are encouraged to work with licensing authorities to preestablish temporary or provisional operating regulations that consider the conditions, challenges, and environment that may be present after a disaster. For example, temporary regulations could account for the potential lack of power or loss of fencing that may occur.

In addition to addressing continuity-of-care issues, the plan must address conducting damage assessments, restoring or rebuilding affected early child-care facilities, and engaging organizations that may be able to provide financial assistance.

For those child-care programs receiving CCDF funding, regulations require that procedures for evacuation, relocation, shelter in place, lockdown, reunification with families, and continuity of operations, among other topics, must be in place. These regulations apply to all organizations receiving CCDF funding, including license-exempt providers. Some states have also chosen to apply these requirements to all child-care providers, regardless of whether they receive CCDF funding or not (Office of Child Care, 2017).

Head Start Requirements

The Head Start program requires emergency-preparedness planning. Head Start and Early Head Start are run by 1,700 agencies across the United States, US territories, and 155 tribal communities. These programs receive federal funding to operate. Each year, these programs provide services to more than a million children aged zero to five. Head Start serves low-income children and families and provides them with early learning education; health and wellness services; and family assistance, such as housing stability, workforce training, and financial stability. Since the program was established in 1965, Head Start has served more than 36 million children (Office of Head Start, 2018c). Federal funding for Head Start and the associated programs (Early Head Start, Migrant and Seasonal Head

Start programs, and so on) was $10,063,095,000 in the fiscal year 2019 (Office of Head Start, 2018b).

Head Start agencies are required to meet the Head Start Program Performance Standards, rules and regulations put forth by the Administration for Children and Families, and the requirements outlined in the Head Start Act of 2007. These requirements include planning, training, and exercising procedures for disasters and emergencies (Office of Head Start, 2018a).

Unfortunately, many times there is a disconnect between the requirements and the day-to-day operations of an early childhood program. This can be for a variety of reasons, but it often boils down to a lack of understanding among preparedness officials, regulators, and the early childhood workforce.

For example, state regulation will require each child-care program to have an emergency plan. However, the majority of early childhood professionals are not emergency-preparedness experts. They create a plan to fulfill the regulation requirement, but often it is not an informed or actionable plan. Then, a licensing inspector will conduct a site visit and will review the plan because it is on the checklist of requirements. Similarly, the inspector is not an emergency-preparedness expert, so the review basically focuses on whether or not a plan exists, not on the quality or practicality of the plan.

This is unfair to all parties: early childhood professionals, inspectors or license-compliance monitors, and the children in our care. To be clear, no one is at fault here. The simple reality is that we can't expect individuals to be emergency-preparedness experts without providing training and resources. One of the goals of this book is to help bridge these disciplines and put these requirements into the early childhood context.

Emergency	Perceived Preparedness	Total Percentage (N=610)
	Not at all/a little	1.63
Fire	Somewhat	7.05
	Ready	91.31
	Not at all/a little	8.69
Tornado	Somewhat	11.80
	Ready	79.34
	Not at all/a little	27.05
Flood	Somewhat	23.93
	Ready	46.72
	Not at all/a little	28.03
Active shooter	Somewhat	26.72
	Ready	45.08

(Leser, Looper-Coats, and Roszak, 2019)

The good news is that there are many benefits to being prepared. Being prepared can positively affect you as an individual, the business that you own or work at, the children in your care, and the families in your community. For instance, FEMA estimates that between 40 and 60 percent of small businesses do not reopen after a disaster (FEMA, n.d.a). Further, there is a direct correlation between the time it takes to reopen and the likelihood of continued operations. Resuming operations as soon as possible is vital. This allows you to resume your cash flow and, importantly, to let your customers know you are open. When businesses are unable to reopen after an emergency, it can have dire consequences. Nearly 90 percent of small businesses that do not reopen within five days of a disaster will fail within a year (FEMA, n.d.a). Additionally, nearly 75 percent of businesses without emergency-preparedness and continuity planning will fail within three years of a disaster (FEMA, n.d.b). These considerations are important to the early childhood community.

The Economic Impact of Child Care

While often overlooked, the early childhood sector contributes a substantial amount of money to the United States economy. In 2012, the child-care industry generated more than $41.5 billion in revenues. The child-care sector aligns with outpatient medical facilities, waste collection, scientific research, and advertising agencies in terms of overall size and economic contribution (Stevens, 2017). The early childhood sector also accounts for another $41.6 billion in indirect output to other sectors, such as real estate, furniture, supplies, and transportation; it represents nearly $1 trillion in economic activity in the United States (Stevens, 2017).

These figures can have compounding impacts at the local level. A study conducted in Missouri in 2013 found that every dollar spent on child care generated $1.87 in spending within the community. This economic boost aided the local economy and helped bolster other local businesses (Schaefer, Gates, and Kiernan, 2013).

Many early childhood programs are small businesses. This is important as small businesses account for 99 percent of all companies and employ 50 percent of all private-sector employees (FEMA, n.d.c). According to data from the 2012 US Economic Census, 768,521 child-care establishments were operating in the country, with 90 percent being classified as family child-care programs or one-person operations (Stevens, 2017; Committee for Economic Development, 2019). While certainly large in quantity, when compared to child-care centers, family child-care providers generated approximately 25 percent of total revenue for the entire early childhood sector. Workforce numbers are difficult to quantify, but several groups estimate at least 12 million children under the age of six are in a child-care arrangement (Stevens, 2017).

These statistics are critical and help paint an important picture for policymakers and professional emergency-management organizations. These facts and figures show the impact of child care as a business. We also need to consider the impact that a lack of child-care services has on a community.

If child care is not available, parents are unable to work. In communities suffering from a disaster, rebuilding and recovery efforts can be delayed when people are not able to rejoin the workforce. Little research has been done about the economic impacts of early childhood closure post-disaster. However, a study looking at the normal breakdowns in child care, such as children being sick, child-care programs temporarily closing, breakdowns in transportation, and other routine events, found that these breakdowns caused families and the overall economy to lose $8.2 billion in wages each year (Glynn and Corley, 2016).

The Role of Child Care in Mitigating Trauma

In addition to the economic consequences of child-care closures, there is also an impact on mental health in disasters. The study of adverse childhood experiences (ACEs) has recently gained more attention among researchers and educators. An ACE is a traumatic event that occurs when a child is between the ages of birth to seventeen (Centers for Disease Control and Prevention [CDC], 2019b). An ACE may be caused by numerous events, such as experiencing violence, residing in a household where there is substance abuse, instability due to family separation, and other events that interfere with a child's safety and stability. ACEs research has shown that these events can cause significant lifelong impacts, including mental health problems, chronic diseases, risk of injury, and sexual abuse and trafficking (CDC, 2019b).

An emergency or disaster could potentially be considered an ACE or create conditions ripe for ACE occurrences. Disasters compound previous problems, and those problems are likely to be even greater after a disaster. Consider the following:

- After the Oklahoma City bombing on April 19, 1995, alcohol consumption was 2.5 times greater in that city than that of similarly situated communities.
- After a devastating tornado hit Joplin, Missouri, in 2001, alcohol use increased 80 percent in Joplin.
- After the attacks on September 11, 2001, the use of anxiety medications increased by 19 percent in New York City (Community Partnership of the Ozarks, n.d.)
- At the beginning of the COVID-19 pandemic, between February 16 and March 15, 2020, prescriptions filled per week for antidepressant, antianxiety, and anti-insomnia medications increased 21 percent (Express Scripts, 2020).

The World Health Organization (WHO) has even stated that severe child abuse may increase after natural disasters (WHO, 2005). Sadly, affected communities have experienced this firsthand. In the six months after Hurricane Floyd hit North Carolina in 1999, there was a fivefold increase in the number of children under two who suffered from inflicted traumatic brain injury. Counties not impacted by the hurricane did not have the same traumatic results (Community Partnership of the Ozarks, n.d.). In addition to the increase in alcohol use, the city of Joplin also experienced a 40 percent increase in domestic violence. Puerto Rico witnessed an uptick in suicides and depression after Hurricane Maria caused widespread damage to the island in 2017. Early childhood professionals in Puerto Rico also reported changed behaviors in children, including increased fear, anxiety, and the inability to concentrate (Region II Head Start Association, 2019).

The conditions during and after an emergency can create an environment ripe for ACEs. To counteract the impacts of ACEs, researchers are now studying positive childhood experiences (PCEs). Though the research is still ongoing, there seem to be promising signs of using PCEs to reverse some of the effects of ACEs (Bethell et al., 2019). Returning children to a normal, safe, and stable environment and predictable routines seems to help mitigate the impacts of ACEs.

Emergency preparedness planning and efforts are directly aligned with this goal. Through our efforts, we want to resume operations and return to normalcy as quickly as possible. Planning, drilling, and exercising our emergency plan allows us to minimize the impact that emergencies and disasters will have on our staff, our finances, our children, and our families. As the research around ACEs and PCEs continues, we will likely learn more about how best to incorporate these principles into our emergency-preparedness planning.

3

Creating an Emergency Plan

All jurisdictions require early childhood programs to create an emergency plan. However, depending on the jurisdiction, some child-care arrangements may be exempt. In certain states, after-school programs, religious organizations, programs below a certain number of enrolled children, or family child-care providers may be subject to all, some, or none of the requirements. However, the trend nationally is to include more child-care arrangements in being subject to emergency-preparedness regulations. In fact, it is certainly possible that some programs that are currently exempt from these requirements will see their exemption rescinded or modified in the coming years.

It is important that the emergency planning process is taken seriously and not performed in a rushed or hurried manner. The more work and attention that can be devoted to creating these plans, the better the outcomes are likely to be. It is also important to set aside time to think about your plans, policies, and procedures during times of calm and normalcy. During times of stress or crisis, it will be difficult to devote the kind of time and attention that these issues merit. As the saying goes, the time to learn how to use a fire extinguisher is not when the building is on fire. The following pages will walk you through what you need to know to create an emergency plan.

What You Need to Know

- Learn the requirements of your jurisdiction.
- Determine local resources that can help you with your plan.
- Understand your community's risk assessment.
- Become familiar with your evacuation site.
- Learn the emergency notification plan.
- Seek training on responding during a disaster.
- Submit your emergency plan for review.

Learn the Requirements of Your Jurisdiction

The first step in creating your plan is to become familiar with the requirements of your jurisdiction. Often you will find these at the state level. The best place to start is with the entity that provides your license to operate. You may need to contact the health department, a social-services agency, the department of education, or a specialized early childhood agency.

Take a moment to read through these requirements to understand what information you are being asked to provide. Also, look to see if a sample plan or template has been provided for your use. Often jurisdictions will make these available, as they help standardize the look and feel of emergency plans. Standardization makes it easier for the inspectors to determine whether or not you have met a requirement. These templates can be useful, but remember they contain the minimum required information. You can certainly add to and build upon the template to ensure you have a comprehensive plan that addresses your needs.

Determine Local Resources That Can Help You with Your Plan

After you have become familiar with the requirements, the next step is to determine local resources that may be able to assist you with the plan. A great resource is your local emergency-management agency. These agencies are government organizations charged with developing and implementing emergency plans for your city, county, or state. Depending on where you live, you may have a local city-based emergency manager, a county-based emergency manager, and/or a state-based emergency manager. Often these agencies are housed within the fire or police department, or they may be a stand-alone agency.

An emergency manager's job is to coordinate disaster response and recovery. This coordination function is important, as it means the manager must be well connected to the community and well aware of the needs and assets that the community has. Emergency managers often determine where the emergency shelters will be located within the community and also can be responsible for equipping and staffing these shelters.

Early childhood professionals serve a vulnerable population, one which requires special considerations during emergencies. Vulnerable populations are very important groups for emergency managers.

In some jurisdictions, it is required that early childhood programs share a copy of their emergency plan with the local emergency-management agency. This requirement offers a chance for emergency management to get to know the early childhood workforce. Also, sharing your plan provides an excellent opportunity to coordinate plans. For example, we conducted training in a community where every program had a plan. None of the plans were coordinated, and none of the programs had ever discussed their plans with each other. When we all came together as a group to discuss the plans, every program had the local library listed as the site where they would relocate to during an emergency. This presented several problems.

First, none of the programs had reached out to the library and asked permission, nor had they made the library aware of this plan. Second, the library was small and had limited capacity. It certainly could not have accommodated all of the children and staff from these various programs. Also, the library did not have a generator, and its policy was to close during an emergency. All of these pieces of information were very important. However, no one had a comprehensive view of how the plans were interconnected until the programs came together. This is why emergency management is necessary.

Understand Your Community's Risk Assessment

Once you have connected with your emergency-management agency, you will need to understand your community's risk assessment. Most communities conduct community risk assessments at regular intervals. These may be called risk assessments, or they may be called Threat and Hazard Identification and Risk Assessments (THIRAs). No matter the name, the purpose is to examine the likelihood of certain types of emergencies or disasters and then provide a ranking for the biggest threats to your particular community. These can be very insightful, especially as you begin thinking about the type of events that may impact your program. Community risk assessments can often be found on the emergency management agency's website.

Other sources of hazard information can include the following:

- The US Geological Survey (USGS): for data on water flow, floods, volcanoes, earthquakes, and landslides (https://www.usgs.gov)
- The National Weather Service (NWS) and its local offices: for information on weather threats such as hurricanes, extreme heat, extreme cold, drought, tornadoes, and historical weather data (https://www.weather.gov)
- The Federal Insurance and Mitigation Administration, which manages the National Flood Insurance Program: for data on floodplains, building codes, and zoning information (https://www.fema.gov/what-mitigation/federal-insurance-mitigation-administration#)
- The US Nuclear Regulatory Commission: for information related to nuclear power plants and evacuation zones (https://www.nrc.gov/about-nrc/emerg-preparedness/about-emerg-preparedness/planning-zones.html)
- Local emergency planning committees: federally required to meet and conduct assessments regarding chemicals and hazardous materials in your local community. They have information about possible hazards a particular community may face, including transportation, manufacturing, and storage

of hazardous materials. (See https://www.epa.gov/epcra/local-emergency-planning-committees)

- US Environmental Protection Agency: hosts numerous databases related to hazardous materials and naturally occurring hazards, such as radon. Radon is an odorless, colorless gas that can cause a wide variety of health effects, including lung cancer. (https://www.epa.gov/radon/epa-map-radon-zones)

In addition to these resources, professional emergency managers usually have historical references as well. These facts and figures can be useful in determining risk. For example, tornadoes are a threat to many places in the United States. While schools across the country plan and practice for tornadoes, these weather events remain a very low threat. In examining records dating back to 1884, tornadoes have only struck occupied schools forty-seven times. Since 1953, a tornado has struck an occupied school only seven times (Total Security Solutions, 2018). We would classify these as a low-occurrence/high-risk events. But, when these seven tornadoes did strike, they caused thousands of injuries and the deaths of 293 students. These events would certainly be classified as having a rare likelihood but severe consequences.

Likelihood	Negligible (no lost time at work or school)	Minor (some lost time at work or school)	Moderate (significant lost time at work or school)	Critical (unable to return to work or school)	Catastrophic (death)
Almost certain	High	High	High	Extreme	Extreme
Likely	Medium	Medium	High	Extreme	Extreme
Possible	Medium	Medium	High	High	Extreme
Unlikely	Low	Medium	Medium	High	High
Rare	Low	Low	Medium	High	High

Risk assessments can be very valuable as a starting point for planning. However, when examining these lists, also keep in mind that some hazards are interrelated. Earthquakes may be a threat in your area. While planning for an earthquake, also consider the other hazards that may occur if an earthquake does happen. For example, an earthquake may also cause power outages, bridge collapses, or even dam failures, possibly leading to floods.

Become Familiar with Your Evacuation Site

Emergency management officials are tasked with developing evacuation plans for the community. They have a deep knowledge of the available resources, including buildings that may be used as emergency shelters. Often, the emergency management agency is the entity that enters into a memorandum of agreements with the emergency shelter locations. These locations may include government-owned facilities such as schools, gyms, convention centers, and sporting event venues. However, some communities also have agreements with private industry, such as warehouses, home-improvement stores, churches, or nonprofit entities within the community. The emergency manager will have specific information about where these sites are located and which ones will serve as primary and secondary sheltering locations.

If you have ever been to an emergency shelter, you know it is not a fun place to be. Many shelter locations are not designed for young children, but these spaces can become more child friendly through the expertise of early childhood professionals. Perhaps the community could create a cache of toys, books, bedding, and supplies that can be stored at the shelter or quickly transported to the shelter in the event of an emergency. Shelters could include a comfortable and safe area for women to breastfeed, and the floors could be made more comfortable for children. Early childhood professionals can review the shelter site for any possible hazards to young children, such as uncovered electrical outlets.

Learn the Emergency Notification Plan

Most of the public school systems in the United States are well connected to the local government and receive the benefit of early notification of emergency incidents. However, many early childhood programs, especially those that are family home-based care or private facilities, have had a difficult time accessing emergency notification systems. Ideally, we would like to see a system where all child-serving institutions receive emergency alerts. This could include alerts about severe weather, police activity in the area, fire and hazardous-materials responses, and even active-shooter incidents. The sooner everyone is notified, the better. Some communities have chosen to invest in mobile alerts, texting, and/or mobile applications to keep their citizens informed. Take the opportunity to discuss the options that are available in your community, and learn how you may be able to access these alerts.

While children are an important consideration for emergency management, we often find that early childhood programs get overlooked. Most emergency managers have strong relationships with the public and private school systems, but we rarely see strong relationships with early childhood providers. Some emergency managers have stated that child care is too difficult to communicate with because we lack a centralized structure. For the benefit of the community, child-care professionals need to have a relationship with emergency management. Further, emergency managers need to recognize and plan for the differences between older children and those served by prekindergarten programs.

Seek Training on Responding during a Disaster

Many emergency-management offices offer training for community members. The Community Emergency Response Team (CERT) program is designed to increase community engagement and train community members on how best to respond during disasters. CERT began in 1985 as an initiative of the Los Angeles City Fire Department and became a federally funded program in 1993. CERT now has programs in all fifty states and has a membership of over six hundred thousand volunteers.

CERT is a formalized curriculum that teaches participants about basic disaster-response skills, such as fire safety, light search and rescue, team organization, and disaster medical operations (FEMA, 2020a). Often, emergency-management agencies use CERT as a public-outreach tool and as a source for volunteers. When large incidents happen, CERT is called to help respond to emergencies and disasters. For more information about CERT opportunities, membership, and trainings, conduct an internet search with the acronym "CERT" and your location/state.

Another resource you may have in your community is the Medical Reserve Corps (MRC). MRC is typically run out of the local health department. MRC is a volunteer program that seeks to bolster emergency response and recovery efforts through the use of trained volunteers. Despite the name, no prior medical training is needed to participate. MRC has nearly one thousand local chapters and approximately two hundred thousand volunteers throughout the United States (Public Health Emergency, 2020). Much like CERT, MRC members receive training and respond to local emergencies and disasters, such as wildfires, hurricanes, tornadoes, blizzards, floods, and public health emergencies.

One of the exciting partnerships that the Institute for Childhood Preparedness has managed to forge is a partnership between these two programs and local early childhood professionals. In some communities, we have conducted meetings where CERT and/or MRC members work with and learn from the pre-K community. For example, one community hosted an evening program where CERT members were paired with child-care providers so that they could help review and revise the emergency plan for the child-care program. In another community, MRC used its funding and expertise to create emergency backpacks for early childhood programs. In addition to the backpacks, early childhood professionals also received basic emergency-preparedness training.

One of the most promising trends I have witnessed is local emergency managers reaching out to the early childhood field to create emergency-response teams. These teams may operate as a branch of the MRC or CERT, but their primary purpose is to care for children during emergencies and disasters. This includes creating a roster of individuals who already work with children, have already completed background checks, and are willing to assist their community in times of crisis.

In addition to being good for the community, this could also serve as a potential revenue source if early childhood programs have to close. FEMA published a disaster-assistance guidance in 2010 addressing public assistance for child-care services in disaster-stricken areas (FEMA, 2010). Under this program, FEMA will reimburse reasonable costs associated with child care during federally declared disasters and emergencies. In addition to helping families, child-care providers can receive compensation for providing child-care services in shelters, so long as the operations are run through the local or state government. Further, costs associated with minor modifications of shelters to enhance the ability to care for children are covered.

The availability of these funding mechanisms is something that child-care resource and referral agencies should become familiar with as they are in a perfect position to partner with local shelters to provide these services. This would benefit all parties: children, families, child-care providers, and those in shelters.

Submit Your Emergency Plan for Review

Emergency-management professionals have vast experience and training in planning for disasters. Some states, such as Arkansas and New Jersey, actually require early childhood programs to submit their emergency plans to the local emergency-management office for review. If your state does not have this requirement, it is still a good idea to reach out to your local emergency manager and see what assistance she would be willing to provide. As government agencies, their services are funded by taxpayer dollars, so it certainly does not hurt to ask.

For some, creating a plan may seem overwhelming, especially when you consider the number of emergencies or disasters that your facility could potentially face. The good news is that a well-designed plan should cover the majority of emergencies that may arise. In the past, there was a feeling that a separate plan was needed for each emergency. As you can imagine, that approach got very confusing and took a lot of time to create a multitude of plans.

The new trend is to create a plan that is "all hazards," which means that your plan should be flexible enough to cover a wide variety of situations. The goal is to have your plan be general enough so that it covers 90–95 percent of situations. This allows for flexibility. While each disaster or emergency is unique, there are certain things that you are going to need to do in every incident. The rest of the plan should deal with the particular challenges faced by a specific hazard. For context, here are some questions that you will need to answer in every situation:

- Who is in charge, and who can make decisions?
- Who will be responsible for communicating with families, the public, and stakeholders?

- How will staff be kept informed of the situation, and how will internal communication be handled?
- What are the expectations of staff?
- If additional help is needed, how and where will that support come from?
- What are our priorities, and who decides how they are communicated?
- Who will determine if you are going to stay or leave the property?
- Who will determine when it is safe to return to normal operations?

This all-hazards approach helps make things simpler and easier to remember in a high-stress situation. This is also useful when training staff, as many of the policies and procedures will be similar, regardless of the emergency. Plans need to provide guidance but not be overbearing or attempt to dictate every action. Emergencies and disasters are unpredictable, and plans must account for this variability.

Similarly, plans should stay away from specifying certain people by name. For example, avoid stating, "Jane will make the decision on whether or not we should evacuate the facility." Instead state, "The decision to evacuate the facility will be made by the director. The lead teacher will make the decision in the event the director is unavailable." This allows your plan to be more flexible. Jane may not always be at work; she may be off-site at a conference or meeting. Further, Jane may not be the director six months from now. Plans should focus tasks based on position, not the individual. This ensures that plans will still be relevant and able to be carried out, even when staff turnover occurs. In some emergency preparedness circles, this is referred to as *continuity*.

4 Communication

Communication is always essential. No matter what type of emergency occurs, there will be a communication component of your plan. The plan should answer questions such as the following:

- How do we receive information about the emergency?
- Who is responsible for reaching out to parents and families?
- What do we say if we receive inquiries?

As communication is a vital part of any emergency, standardize this section and follow it during each incident.

Communication is the single biggest point of failure in an emergency or disaster. It is an essential service and one that requires training and testing. Communication encompasses a wide variety of actions: internal communication, stakeholder communication, parental communication, media communication, and staff communication, just to name a few.

The ability to communicate in emergencies is crucial for the rapid response of emergency responders and the accountability to friends and family. Communication is key so that members of society remain calm and can comprehend the situation at hand. All audiences will want information regarding the situation; therefore, it is key to develop a crisis communications plan before an emergency. Communications should be able to reach various audiences with information specific to their concerns and needs. Compile the contact information for each audience you will need to contact and inform. Audiences may consist of enrolled families, suppliers, management, government officials, employees, the community, and the media (FEMA, 2016). Keep this information in a database that is immediately accessible during an emergency. Lists should be updated regularly and are to remain confidential.

In all of these types of communications, strive for unity of messaging. *Unity of messaging* means that you are putting out similar and nonconflicting information for both internal and external use. In today's society, information moves rapidly. It is incumbent on our organizations to ensure that the information presented is timely and accurate. This leads to trust and credibility.

Society has become more reliant on technology, including social media as well as cell phones, for day-to-day communications. Keep in mind that cell phone towers are often overwhelmed during large-scale disasters. Data from recent disasters highlight this point:

- During Hurricane Katrina, there was almost complete disruption with more than 60 percent of cell towers still down three weeks after the event (Leitl, 2006).
- During Superstorm Sandy, 25 percent of cell towers failed (CBS News, 2012).
- During Hurricane Maria, 95 percent of cell towers failed, with 84 percent still down three weeks after the event (Caron, 2017; Sullivan and Schwartz, 2018).

These percentages stress the need for a multimodal communication strategy, one that includes traditional communication methods such as landline phones, telephone calling trees (where one person is responsible for passing the message to others), and cell phones. This strategy also includes new media communication methods, such as email, Facebook, Twitter, Instagram, and mobile texting. For starters, consider these questions:

- Is communication covered in your plan?
- How will you communicate with parents in your program?
- What happens if the phones are down? Do you have back-up plans?
- Have you tested these systems?
- Has the plan been provided to parents?
- Which staff are responsible for parent communication?
- Which staff are responsible for reunification of children with their families?
- How are you maintaining up-to-date contact information for the families in your program?
- How often are your records updated?

Through our planning, we want to ensure we are able to successfully communicate to customers and handle the crisis in an organized fashion. Crises are unpredictable, and safety is a top priority in every emergency; therefore, it is critical to relay the details to all parties involved to minimize negative impacts.

These seven tips can aid your facility in better communication:

1. **Respond quickly.** Families will expect an immediate response to any circumstance when their children's safety is at risk. If this is not accomplished, families will jump to conclusions that may harm your business and hinder the organization of your action plan. The longer an issue goes unresolved, the more restless and concerned the public becomes.

2. **Leverage your supporters.** Establish a community before an emergency strikes. By establishing a strong audience, it will be easier to achieve resilience, and investing interest and understanding in your stakeholders will make them more apt to support your families and facility in times of need.

3. **Put the victims first.** No matter the circumstances, it is always about the victims—not about your business. Acknowledge the circumstances the victims are in, and provide support and/or a sincere apology. Refusal to take responsibility or give support can damage your rapport and foster mistrust within the community.

4. **Don't play the blame game.** If you put your assets toward blaming who is at fault, you are putting your business before the victim. Assess the crisis, handle it appropriately, and take care of the victims.

5. **Be transparent.** Think of what the families and community want to know about the crisis. Always provide truthful answers, and be willing to be vulnerable to the public. You are under a microscope amid a crisis, so being forthright—whether positive or negative—saves hassle and can facilitate a smoother recovery for all parties.

6. **Perform "What if?" work.** Despite the unpredictability of most emergency circumstances, try your best to prepare for possible scenarios by anticipating the situation and modeling a plan for how to handle it. Focus on situations that have a high likelihood of impacting your business. Remember to center your plan on aiding the families and community. Communicating your practice efforts will establish trust between your facility and the community and will make you better equipped if the situation does occur.

7. **Make sure your message is consistent company wide.** Ensure your staff is on the same page so that you can respond to a crisis collectively. For instance, write up a simple paper that outlines each department's actions, and share it throughout your business to foster cohesiveness for your facility and the community (FEMA, 2020b).

Learning about the Emergency or Disaster

The US Department of Homeland Security provides various methods of communication to the public in emergencies, such as Wireless Emergency Alerts (WEAs) via the Integrated Public Alert and Warning System (IPAWS), the Emergency Alert System (EAS), and the National Oceanic and Atmospheric Administration (NOAA) Weather Radio (NWR) (FEMA, 2020b).

Wireless Emergency Alerts

WEAs are received on your mobile/cell phone and are similar to text messages. Unlike text messages, WEAs are designed to grab attention and alert the public with sound and vibration, both repeated twice. WEAs are sent by state and local public-safety officials, the NWS, the National Center for Missing and Exploited Children, and the president of the United States. These messages are no more than ninety characters long; are free of charge; and will include information such as the type and time of the alert, actions to be taken, and the agency issuing the alert. WEAs will fall into three alert categories: imminent threat, America's Missing: Broadcast Emergency Response (AMBER), and presidential (FEMA, 2020b).

Emergency Alert System

Similarly, the EAS system is a national public warning system that broadcasts wide-scale messages to the public via broadcasters, satellite digital audio service, direct broadcast satellite providers, cable television systems, and wireless cable systems. The system provides the president with the capability to address the American public within ten minutes of a national emergency. This system may also be utilized by state and local authorities to broadcast urgent weather notifications, imminent threats, AMBER alerts, and local incident information targeted to specific areas. The president has sole authority to dictate when the national-level EAS will be activated. FEMA is responsible for national-level EAS tests. When other means of public communication are not viable, the government will resort to EAS (FEMA, 2020b).

NOAA Weather Radio

NWR is a network of more than seven hundred fifty broadcast transmitters that cover over 90 percent of the United States (National Weather Service, n.d.b). These stations broadcast continuous weather information nationwide from the nearest National Weather Service office. The NWR broadcasts official weather warnings, watches, forecasts, and other hazards twenty-four hours a day, seven days a week. This system can also be used to broadcast alerts of nonweather-related emergencies, such as threats to national security and natural, environmental, and public safety. The NWR can be found on frequencies between 162.400 and 162.550 megahertz. You can access these frequencies via any NOAA Weather Radio and also on a variety of walkie-talkies. For a map showing broadcast areas and frequencies, see https://www.weather.gov/mob/nwr

Other Communication Platforms

On the local level, there will typically be opt-in text and email systems, Enhanced Telephone Notification (ETN) systems, local school or organization notification systems, and outdoor sirens to provide immediate communication efforts. Apps such as the FEMA app, American Red Cross app, the Weather Channel app, and more are also available on individual cellular devices (FEMA, 2020b).

Further, many local municipalities have established mechanisms for citizens to receive emergency alerts. A popular platform is called CodeRED by OnSolve. This platform allows for real-time emergency alerts on your cell phone. CodeRed has been implemented in thousands of communities throughout the United States (OnSolve, 2020). Your local jurisdiction may use CodeRED or a similar system. To find out which system is available in your area, perform an internet search with the name of your city and "emergency alert system."

Additionally, all child-care facilities should have a battery-operated AM/FM radio. This ensures you can receive the latest information regardless of whether electricity is available. Each state has radio stations designed to serve as the primary relay stations for emergency alerts. You may recall that this system was called the Emergency Broadcast System up until 1997, when it was replaced with EAS. Each state has a formal emergency alert system state plan, which describes how the system is operated, activated, and tested.

Embracing new technologies is key to communication. This helps our early childhood programs show value to our customers. For example, recent studies have indicated that only around 15 percent of emails are opened, whereas 98 percent of text messages are read—95 percent within the first three minutes (Doherty, 2014; Dudley, 2020; Olensky, 2013). You have likely heard from families that texting is becoming a preferred way of communicating. In addition to being easy and efficient, texting offers some advantages over the traditional landline or cell-phone calling. First, you can often send text messages when you are unable to place calls. Because text messages are small pieces of data, they are easier to receive and transmit than voice calls, which require more bandwidth. Further, with texting, you can communicate to a wide number of individuals all at once without the need to manually dial each individual. Mobile texting systems have matured over time. Many early childhood programs are using texting as a method of communication for both routine matters, such as picture day, tuition payments, and field trips, and emergencies.

During a disaster, communication networks such as cell phones and computers, as well as electricity, may be unreliable or overtaxed. Planning can help minimize disruptions. The following are simple steps you can take to create your communication plan:

- Obtain contact information and ensure it is updated regularly. Phone numbers for your staff and your customers can change. Develop policies and procedures that account for this reality. At a minimum, obtain phone numbers twice a year. Due to turnover and change, however, it is a good idea to request this information more frequently—at least once a quarter.

- Utilize technology to make accessing your information more efficient. There are a lot of online services that can store information securely. Google, Dropbox, Apple, Amazon, and others offer cloud-based storage. Having contact information available both in paper form and online can be helpful, especially if you have to leave your facility in a hurry. Some directors email the contact information to themselves. This way, it's in their in-box if needed.

- In addition to the information for your staff and families, be sure plans contain the contact information for vital community services and partners. These include emergency services, medical facilities, schools, the poison control center, child-care licensing officials, the local health department, utility service providers, transportation companies, and providers of other services that you may need in an emergency.

- Encourage staff members to share their contact information with each other, as it may be the only way everyone can communicate during a disaster, especially if staff members or classroom groups become separated. Available technology easily allows for contact information to be stored in mobile devices.

Other tips to keep in mind when using communication devices during an emergency:

- When possible, use text messaging, email, or social media rather than phone calls, as these methods use less bandwidth and may work better when phone service is disrupted.
- Keep conversations brief, and convey only vital information; this will also help save your cell phone's battery life.
- Store extra batteries and a charger for mobile devices in an emergency kit. Solar power, crank, or vehicle phone chargers or prepaid cell phones are optimal.
- Update contact lists frequently on phones, in email, and in other channels.
- Save safe meeting locations on a phone's mapping application.
- Conserve the cellular battery by reducing screen brightness and closing unused apps.
- Wait at least ten seconds to redial after a failed call and avoid downloads to reduce network congestion (Government of Canada, 2015).

Family Communication Plans

Encourage families in your program to also develop emergency-preparedness plans. Creating a family emergency communication plan is relatively easy, and many templates currently exist online. An easy-to-use template can be found at the Sesame Street in Communities website, https://sesamestreetincommunities. org/topics/emergency-preparedness/

A comprehensive plan should include all phone numbers and information every family member may need in any given emergency. Families should ensure that every family member has a copy. If normal communication, such as text messaging or calling, is overloaded or out of power, have a contingency plan for getting ahold of everyone. Make sure that each family member has a mode of communication, whether is a cellular device, a landline at work or school, or reporting to a prearranged meet-up area. Obviously, this will not be practical for younger children, so families should ensure they are familiar with the child-care program or school's emergency plans.

It is also important to establish an out-of-state, in-case-of-emergency (ICE) contact. Every family member should feel comfortable reaching out to the contact, as this person will serve as a coordinator. The contact likely will not be directly affected by the disaster, so it will be easier for the person to provide, receive, and relay information. During disasters, it is sometimes easier to call out of state than it is to call across town. There are bandwidth issues during disasters, because everyone is trying to make calls at the same time. Ensure all family members know the plan and that everyone is aware of the ICE contact's information (US Marine Corps, n.d.).

Helping Children Stay Informed

Children should be taught their names, addresses, parents' or guardians' names, and phone numbers at an early age. This information is vital during emergencies, especially if children get separated from families or early childhood professionals. Simple conversations with children can help them learn this information, for example: "We just arrived home. Can you tell me our address?" "Daddy will be home soon. Can you tell me his name?"

For those unable to speak or unable to comprehend this information, some early childhood programs have created T-shirts. These T-shirts are worn during tornado warnings and watches and other types of emergencies. They contain the child's name, address, phone number, and any medication or allergy information. The shirts are often brightly colored, which enables the children to be spotted more easily if they are separated from the group.

Communicating the Need for Help

Time is of the essence during an emergency or a disaster. Yet, we often see early childhood programs that are reluctant to empower their staff to call 911 during an emergency. Some programs have a policy that only the director can call 911 and request emergency services. Generally speaking, policies like these are foolish. They waste time and can delay life-saving help from arriving.

Directors are encouraged to empower their staff by clearly establishing guidelines related to summoning emergency assistance. There are a wide variety of scenarios that would dictate the need for staff to call 911 immediately, such as an individual choking, an unconscious person, severe bleeding, a hostile act or the threat of a hostile act, or a utility failure such as a gas leak. These are but a few examples of how a delay in notification to the director would be counterproductive.

Further, staff must know how to call 911. Post emergency numbers by each landline in your program. Also include the street address of your program, and ensure all staff know and can recite your address from memory. There are major differences between calling 911 from a landline, a mobile device, and voice-over-internet-protocol (VOIP). Reaching emergency services from a landline is the quickest way to ensure information is transmitted in a timely manner. Landlines use enhanced 911 systems, which automatically transmit information about the name, location, police beat, and nearest fire and EMS units to dispatch when a call is made. The information transmits automatically, regardless of whether the caller is able to speak or not. The biggest pitfall of using a landline phone is that many phone systems require the user to dial a predetermined number or code to reach an outside line. For example, some systems require the user to dial 9 before receiving an outside line. In these cases, a user would need to dial 9911 to reach emergency services. If this is the case in your facility, be sure you post this information conspicuously near the landline phone.

Cell-phone technology is in a constant state of flux. New models, new technologies, and even new networks are constantly being built. Emergency 911 centers are working to keep up with these changes, but, as of now, they are a bit behind. The information obtained by 911 operators varies greatly depending on the age of the cell phone and the cellular provider that the caller uses. In some cases, the dispatch center will receive actual GPS coordinates, based off of the GPS sensors in the cell phone. In other cases, the dispatch center will receive an approximate location based off of triangulation data from the nearest cell phone towers. In nearly all cases, it is very unlikely that dispatch will receive the actual address of the location of the cell phone. Therefore, child-care program staff must know the physical address of their workplace.

As of the writing of this book, there is not widespread adoption of text to 911, meaning that texting to 911 during an emergency is not a reliable method of communication. This is expected to change over the next several years, as many jurisdictions are testing or implementing systems that allow individuals to send text messages to 911 (Federal Communications Commission, n.d.). Likewise, many emergency dispatch centers are currently not equipped to receive photos and videos via multimedia messaging service (MMS).

Critical Documents

Ensuring access to critical documents during an emergency can be important. Recent studies have shown that more than half of Americans do not have back-up copies of crucial documents, such as insurance paperwork, emergency contact lists, staffing lists, registration/enrollment data, contact information for parents and guardians, and titles to vehicles and property (Quadir, 2012). For some organizations, this can also include financial records or even personal items such as passports, birth certificates, or Social Security cards.

Early childhood programs are encouraged to save important data twice and in two different locations. Luckily, storage and access to a cloud backup has never been easier, and a wide variety of low-cost options exist for ensuring data is backed up and accessible. Further, technology has enabled programs to store large amounts of data with great ease. For this reason, many are not only including paper-based information but also photographic information, such as pictures of enrolled children and families and photos of classrooms, furniture, equipment, and supplies. These photographs come in handy for family-reunification purposes or for insurance claims.

5 Responding to Infectious Disease Outbreaks and Other Disasters

Infectious Disease

Many infectious diseases impact the "bookends" of society: the very young and the very old. As such, extra precautions may be needed to protect our clientele. This may include the temporary closure of our programs, discontinuing group play, limiting the amount and type of toys that children play with, and implementing more stringent cleaning protocols, especially of commonly touched surfaces. Likewise, there are important staffing considerations that must be addressed.

Illness and disease are part of life; consequently, we must ensure we are prepared for handling these types of events. Young children spend countless hours playing, crawling, and discovering. In addition to these activities, children also spend a lot of time touching surfaces and toys. They frequently touch their eyes, noses, and mouths. Unfortunately, these behaviors can lead to an increase in disease spread and transmission.

Much like the rest of their young bodies, a child's immune system is constantly evolving and developing. In addition to the developing immune system, public health interventions, such as hygiene practices, food-safety regulations, proper nutrition, and vaccinations, help protect children. Simple steps, such as having staff and children wash their hands regularly, can help prevent the spread of disease. Infections in child-care settings are most commonly transmitted by contaminated hands; therefore, frequent handwashing is vital (NRCKids.org, 2020).

- **VIRUS:** a microscopic organism that may cause disease. Viruses can contain either DNA or RNA and reproduce in living cells. Viruses spread by using living cells to multiply. Examples include the common cold, chicken pox, rabies, herpes, measles, Ebola, HIV, hepatitis, severe acute respiratory syndrome (SARS), and Middle East respiratory syndrome (MERS) (Healthline Media, 2020).

- **COMMUNICABLE OR CONTAGIOUS:** for our purposes, these words can be used interchangeably. These terms refer to the ability of a disease to be spread or transmitted.

- **SOCIAL DISTANCING:** a public health term used to describe one method of stopping the spread of an infectious disease. The term means maintaining physical distance from others and also avoiding congregate settings. In practice, this means limiting the number of people who are able to gather at any given place or location (Santa Clara County Public Health Department [SCCPHD], n.d.).

- **ISOLATION:** the act of separating an individual who is sick from those who are not sick

- **QUARANTINE:** separating an individual or group of individuals who may have been exposed to a disease or illness. These individuals are not currently showing any signs or symptoms of being sick. Quarantine is used in cases when we do not know whether a person is infected (SCCPHD, n.d.).

- **ENDEMIC:** the amount of disease that is normally found in a community. This can be considered the baseline level of disease (CDC, 2012).

- **EPIDEMIC:** when the amount of disease in a given area rises, often suddenly, above the normal (or endemic) level (CDC, 2012)

- **OUTBREAK:** an epidemic in a limited geographic area, such as a neighborhood, city, or county (CDC, 2012)

- **PANDEMIC:** an epidemic that has large reach and impact. Normally, pandemics refer to epidemics that have spread to a large number of individuals. This could include several countries or even an entire continent (CDC, 2012).

Universal Procedures

In the event of an infectious disease event at your school or program, there are some universal procedures that you will want to put into place. First, attempt to isolate the sick individual from the rest of the group. Many programs have established policies and procedures for handling sick individuals, and most have a designated room or area for those who are sick. If the sick individual is a child, it will be important to have a staff member stay with the child until a parent or guardian is able to pick up the child. If the sick individual is a staff member, the staff member should be sent home.

Depending on the type of outbreak, the establishment of daily health screening may be necessary. The purpose of a daily health screening is to ensure sick individuals are not exposing others and spreading disease. Health screenings require participation from families and staff to be most effective. Depending on the situation, the local health department and/or child-care licensing may be also involved. There are a few considerations when establishing a health screening program.

- Families and staff should be provided with information about the current situation. This should include a summary of the disease and the signs/symptoms of those who are ill. It is also wise to provide families with a list of steps that you are taking to protect children and minimize the spread of the illness.
- Emphasize the importance of staying home when sick. This includes families and staff members alike. If a parent notices her child is experiencing signs or symptoms, then the child should remain at home. Likewise, if a staff member is sick, she should not report to work.
- If the situation warrants daily health screenings, you would require staff and children to undergo a health screening before being admitted into the school or program. The health screener would look for signs/symptoms and may also ask questions concerning potential contact with sick or infected individuals.
- Implement procedures to deal with staff or children who become sick on-site.
- Establish clear criteria on when the sick individual may return to the program. As each disease is different, these criteria will need to be flexible and take into account the specifics of the particular illness or disease. Some programs may require a doctor's note before granting reentry into the program or school.

The Basics of Disease Transmission

Diseases have different levels of transmissibility. These are referred to as R_0 (pronounced "R naught"). The R_0 number is a measure of how contagious a particular infectious disease agent is. It reflects the number of secondary cases that one case would be expected to produce. This number is used by public health professionals to help understand how easily spread a particular disease may be and to inform the public health response needed to control an epidemic, outbreak, or pandemic (Delamater et al., 2019). The higher the R_0 value, the more likely the spread. Data such as hospital admissions, new cases of infection, and deaths are used to determine the R_0. The R_0 will fluctuate over time, especially as individuals who were sick recover and have immunity and as public health measures, such as isolation, quarantine, and social distancing take effect. The goal is to drive the R_0 below 1, which will cause the outbreak to subside, as there will not be enough new individuals infected to continue the outbreak.

Depending on how easily a disease spreads, you may need to implement additional procedures at your program. This could include modifying pickup and drop-off policies, lowering the number of children served, lowering the teacher-child ratios, limiting group activities, or even temporarily closing your program. Public health powers in the United States are strongest at the state level, and governors, through their state health departments, are likely to implement new rules, regulations, or orders based on the severity of the situation. As public health powers are vested at the state level, this means there will likely be a state-by-state approach to dealing with a disease. If your program is located close to state borders or serves children from different states, this may complicate your operations.

Each year, new diseases and new strains of diseases are identified, and these new strains pose a challenge to the medical and public health community. In the case of a new, or novel, disease human beings do not have any natural immunity. Further, viruses *mutate, shift,* and *drift*; the body's immune system may not be prepared to handle the changes.

- **Mutation:** a change to the genetic makeup of a virus
- **Drift:** a small change to the genetic makeup of a virus
- **Shift:** a large change to the genetic makeup of a virus

This is the reason why we need a flu shot each year. The normal seasonal influenza is an RNA-based virus. RNA-based viruses are known for mutations. Part of the reason we receive a new flu shot each year is because the anticipated strain of the flu has likely changed from the prior year. A vaccine provides a best guess at which strains of flu will be circulating so that the body can build up some antibodies and immunity to the flu. Some years, the vaccine is a good match; other years, the vaccine is not a good match (CDC, 2020).

One of the threats from a new disease is that the human body will not have any natural immunity to fight the disease off. Further, it takes time for scientists to develop a new vaccine. During this period, public health officials will rely on nonpharmaceutical interventions (NPIs) to help control the spread of disease. NPIs are public health measures that are put in place to help slow the spread of an illness. At the most basic level, NPIs serve to keep people away from one another. If people are not together, then illness cannot readily spread (CDC, 2019a). Historically, examples of NPIs include closing schools, suspending large events such as sports and concerts, limiting the number of individuals in a certain place, and even closing nonessential businesses.

Preparation for an Outbreak

To best prepare for an infectious disease outbreak, early childhood programs are encouraged to establish strong relationships with their local public health department. The public health department can provide a wide variety of resources, technical expertise, and guidance on ways to limit the spread of infectious disease. Further, licensing regulations may require mandatory reporting of infectious disease outbreaks.

In the event of a highly contagious disease outbreak, child-care programs should brace for the possibility of being shuttered for an extended period of time. This may be due to government action or to a decrease in demand for services as parents are asked to work from home or are impacted by nonessential-business closures. Each state has different policies and procedures regarding what businesses are and are not essential, and it is important to understand where your program falls on the list. In some cases, only programs serving essential workers may be allowed to operate. In other cases, programs may be asked to temporarily reduce ratios and limit classroom size. Preparing for these realities and discussing with your insurance carrier what would and would not be covered during a business interruption is of paramount importance.

Ensure you have an established policy on cleaning, sanitizing, and disinfecting. In some cases, a new disease may be so infectious that only professional decontamination organizations are recommended. Establishing a relationship with an entity that can provide deep-cleaning and disinfecting services prior to an outbreak is important. Cleaning supplies and personal protective equipment, such as gloves, tissues, soap, masks, and hand sanitizer, may be in short supply during an outbreak. Make sure you have a supply of these items on hand. You may even consider purchasing extra, so you have them if supply-chain issues arise.

Other Disasters

Of course, there are many other possible disasters that can affect us and the children and families we serve: severe weather, earthquakes, floods, and more. As we explore the following situations, challenge yourself and your staff to think through worst-case scenarios. Be honest about the current capabilities of your staff as well as the limitations related to the program size, location, and funding.

Go/No Go

In a time of crisis, knowing how to handle a situation can be the line between life and death. Therefore, it is key to know the difference between sheltering in place, evacuation, and lockdown. The terminology is often mixed up, and technical definitions, procedures, and training vary by jurisdiction. Often decisions to stay or go can be complicated. The following section provides guidance to aid your decision making.

Sheltering in Place

The purpose of *sheltering in place* is to provide you with physical separation from something hazardous in the outdoor environment. As a general rule of thumb for early childhood programs, the best default is to stay within your facility. This is the space you are most familiar with, a space designed specifically for children and a comfortable environment for them. It is integral to properly stock and equip your facility so that you are well prepared to handle these events. The majority of states specify the emergency supplies that should be on hand. At a minimum, flashlights, drinking water, blankets (if in a cold climate), and a first-aid kit should be on hand and available.

Kids' Galaxy in Gwinnett County, Georgia, serves as a prime example of remaining in your facility or sheltering in place. Janna Rookis, a consultant with Kids' Galaxy, was prepared for a major ice storm and knew sheltering in place was the best option according to the circumstances. Rookis used their center's preexisting checklist to get ready and maintained adequate communication with families via Facebook and the internet while remaining calm and keeping all the children safe through the night. During the ice storm, buses from other districts were out on the road past midnight, and over twelve hundred accidents occurred. Kids' Galaxy avoided this by simply staying within their premises (Institute for Childhood Preparedness, 2019b).

Sheltering in place is used for a wide variety of emergencies:

- **Severe weather:** tornadoes, sudden ice storms, or heavy snow storms
- **Some environmental hazards:** earthquakes, dangerous smoke from a wildfire, chemical contamination, radiation incidents
- **Local emergencies:** short-duration utility outages

Going outside or trying to evacuate in these situations would put personal health and safety at risk; therefore, staying put is the best option. Shelter-in-place situations can take various forms. For some of the more severe threats, such as tornadoes, chemical contamination, dangerous smoke, or radiation incidents, it will be important to move children and staff into the center of the building. Put as many solid walls as possible between the threat and you, your staff, and the children. For shelter-in-place situations that are less severe, such as short-duration power outages, students and staff may be more comfortable remaining in their normal classrooms.

To successfully shelter in place, please keep in mind the following:

- Remain calm.
- Once the decision is made, act quickly.
- Close and/or lock all exterior doors and windows.
- If sheltering in place due to a chemical release or hazardous-materials situation, turn off all heating, cooling, and ventilation systems.
- Move toward the innermost room, and avoid exterior windows.
- Monitor your emergency radio or television for further updates.
- Do not leave your shelter-in-place site until you receive the "all clear" from authorities.

In some cases, however, sheltering in place may not be the safest option. Be sure you and your staff understand evacuations and lockdowns so that you and your child-care facility are prepared if these responses are needed.

Evacuation

Evacuating is exiting a space when there is a direct threat to the health and safety of individuals in that space. The ultimate goal of an evacuation is that individuals in harm's way may move a safe distance from the hazard to ensure personal safety. In some situations, there is a clear chain of command and there are clearly labeled routes and exits; however, in other scenarios, you may be the one leading the evacuation efforts for others. Tension and stress will be high, so as a child-care professional, it essential for you to remain as calm as possible and to model your expectations to the children entrusted to your care.

When are some times you should evacuate?

- Natural gas leaks
- High carbon monoxide levels
- Structural damage to the building (perhaps from an earthquake)
- Wildfires approaching your facility
- Tsunami warnings
- Hazardous chemicals spilled in or nearby your facility
- Fire in your facility

Your child-care program should be equipped for an evacuation. This includes ensuring communication systems and methods are clearly understood by all. Programs should utilize a warning system that is audible throughout the entire building. This could be intercoms, walkie-talkies, group texts, air horns—whatever will ensure that all staff members of your program are alerted. When considering your communication strategies, keep in mind that loud noise may frighten children, which could add to the complexity of evacuating. As with everything, ensuring children are aware of the evacuation procedure, if they are old enough to understand, is important as it helps them to remain calm.

To exit quickly and safely, sufficient exits should be available and unobstructed at all times and in multiple locations. Every room should have at least two ways out. These exits are likely already identified, due to fire-code and licensing requirements. We refer to these exits as primary, secondary, and tertiary. The primary exit is your first choice and likely is the exit you use the majority of the time. This may be a door that leads outside into the playground or parking-lot area. The secondary exit may be another door or even a window that can be opened or broken. Some places will also have a tertiary, or third, exit. For example, you may have a door that leads to your playground that is the primary means of how you get outside. You may also have a door to the hallway or a window that could be broken as a tertiary exit. Knowing your exits is important. It is always a good idea to identify potential exits wherever you are, even if you are just at a restaurant for dinner or at a movie theater to catch a show.

In anticipation of evacuation, put together an emergency-preparedness backpack ahead of time, and hang it by the door, ready to go. Depending on the size of your classroom, one or more bags may be necessary. Ensure these backpacks can be easily located and carried. Items for your emergency-preparedness backpack or "go-bag" may be regulated by your licensing authority. Check to make sure you have the proper supplies on hand, such as the following:

- Water
- Snacks
- Adhesive bandages
- Medical tape
- List of student medications
- Contact information for the families
- Attendance sheets
- Small comfort toys, such as stuffed animals or crayons and paper

This go-bag may be in addition to your larger emergency-preparedness kit.

To maximize your odds of a successful evacuation, consider the following:

- Develop a preplanned route for each room in your building.
- Move away from the hazard at all times.
- Help guide others to safety, if it is safe for you to do so.
- Call 911 when you are safe.
- Follow the instructions of law enforcement or other authorities.

More than half of all families do not have a designated meeting place in case of a disaster. Be sure to share your plan for evacuation and family reunification with the families you serve. Following a major disaster, telephone lines will likely be down or jammed, making it hard to find loved ones. For example, after the earthquake hit Haiti in January 2010, many children and families became separated and had no way of contacting loved ones or knowing whether their family members were alright.

When thinking of evacuation, it is wise to identify a few different meeting places ahead of time. We call these "near sites" and "far sites." One meeting place can be located close to your child-care program. This near site can be used for sudden small emergencies, such as fires. The second site, the far site, should be farther away. The far site serves as a meeting location in case the neighborhood is unsafe, such as during a gas leak. Distance will make evacuation to the far site more difficult and may require transportation. Be sure to think through transportation options ahead of time. A local school, bus company, or families and staff with large vehicles could be transportation options.

Lockdown

Shelter in place and *lockdowns* can often be confused. It is understandable, as they share many of the same traits; however, they are different. A lockdown should be used when there is a risk of hostile activity, such as an armed intruder. An intruder could be any visitor who poses a perceived threat to the safety and welfare of children or staff. In the context of early childhood programs, such an intruder could be a parent or family member of a child who is unauthorized to see the child or be on the premises, a complete stranger with the intent to do harm to children, or a disgruntled former employee or worker previously affiliated with the program. Any kind of situation in which a person makes program staff fearful for their safety or the safety of the children falls into this category. A lockdown can also be used for situations in which an intruder is not on-site at your center but is at large, dangerous, and potentially armed in the community. For example, a prisoner breaking out of policy custody or armed robbers on the loose would be reasons for a lockdown.

The goal of a lockdown is to create a secure location that serves as a safe barrier from the threat. The lockdown should also serve to raise the awareness levels of all the adults. We need them to be our eyes and ears during this time. Our efforts are aimed at physically preventing the threat from entering our space. Performing a successful lockdown includes locking doors and windows, remaining out of sight, and barricading yourself and children in preestablished areas. Normally, situations that warrant a lockdown will require the intervention of law enforcement to help manage or eliminate the threat.

Programs should consider the following key recommendations to implement a successful lockdown:

- o All members of the building staff need to understand, support, and participate in lockdown procedures.
- o The lockdown procedures should be practiced several times per year, similar to fire drills.

- Families should receive lockdown information at enrollment and should be notified of drills and events, in addition to receiving tools to help children cope with disasters.
- Predesignated alternate pickup sites must be shared with families in the event of evacuation after a lockdown. Families should stay away from the facility during a lockdown, as no one will be allowed in or out of the facility.

At first sight or recognition of an intruder, staff should be alert and empowered to act. Whether it's front-desk administrative staff or others who identify the threat, they should call 911 immediately. If a weapon is present, the staff should not engage the person but perhaps offer a hand signal or other notification so other staff can call 911. If the person does not have a weapon, staff should calmly introduce themselves, ask how they can be of assistance, and ask the person, in a nonconfrontational way, to follow the visitors' procedure guidelines. If the individual refuses to follow the program's procedures, staff should not confront but should call 911.

If the unauthorized person makes it through the front-desk waiting area or enters other areas of the building without authorization to do so, staff should quickly alert all on the premises that an intruder is in the building and should begin lockdown procedures. Staff should quickly check halls, restrooms, and outdoors and ensure all children are inside classrooms. Staff should also lock doors, cover windows, and turn off lights to create the appearance of an empty room. Adults and children should be out of sight and hidden in closets, against walls, on the ground, or behind structures that obstruct from outside view. It is important for staff and children to practice maintaining a calm environment. Staff should ensure children know that during such scenarios being very quiet is important. Staff should stay in lockdown position until emergency response or police arrive on scene and/or provide direction that it is "all clear" and safe.

Upon arrival, police in coordination with the program director may decide to evacuate the building. Or, they may decide to resume normal activities on the premises. Either way, families should be alerted of any drills or actual lockdowns as soon as they can be. Directors must also report the incident to licensors.

To perform a successful lockdown, keep in mind the following:

- Remain calm.
- Move to your designated safe spot.
- Lock all doors and windows.
- Barricade the opening to your classroom by using items such as chairs, desks, bookshelves, cots, and tables.
- Become invisible. Turn off all lights, silence all cell phones, reduce or eliminate outside visibility by closing blinds, help children stay quiet, and move as far as possible from the points of entry.
- Keep children quiet and calm. Perhaps use silent toys set aside for emergency situations or kept in your emergency bag that can keep their attention.

- Be prepared to take further action.
- Remain in lockdown until you receive the "all clear" from authorities.

Reunification

During an emergency, it may become necessary to reunite children with their families. The goal of any reunification process is to ensure the safe, orderly, and documented reunion of children with their parents or guardians. These reunifications happen under stressful conditions, so the more staff and families are familiar with the procedures, the better. There will also likely be many different competing demands and priorities during an emergency; having a practiced system in place can help provide familiarity and stability.

On many occasions, it is possible that reunification may occur off-site at an unfamiliar place. Maintaining control of and accountability for all children is a top priority. Also, many vehicles may be swarming the area—first responders, news media, worried parents, curious onlookers, and so on. In the midst of the chaos, make sure that children are released to the appropriate parents or guardians. Having a process in place makes this easier and also provides documentation to help ensure that every child is accounted for and the chain of custody for each child is maintained.

The following example policy provides additional information.

POLICY ON FAMILY REUNIFICATION

PURPOSE: This plan describes the reunification process that we will use in the event that parents or guardians need to pick up their children after an emergency or disaster has occurred. Our goal is to provide a process that ensures the safe, orderly, and documented reunion of children with their parents or guardians.

- **PRE-EVENT NOTIFICATION TO FAMILIES: Upon enrollment in our program, families will be provided information related to our reunification procedure. Families will be asked to fill out a form that details the contact information for the family, as well as a list of individuals authorized to pick up the child. We will discuss with the families our normal pickup procedure and how our procedure in an emergency or disaster may differ. As emergency contact information can change, we ask that families notify us of any changes in contact information or in authorized individuals. Twice a year, we will also ask families to update this information.**

- PLAN ACTIVATION: The family reunification plan will be activated by the director or her designee. The activation should occur as soon as possible after an incident occurs that warrants reunification. The safety of staff and children is paramount, and those efforts designed to save and protect life take priority. Once the director or designee decides to activate the plan, staff members should be notified in person or by walkie-talkie or cell phone.

- REUNIFICATION PROCESS: During an emergency or disaster, stress levels will be high. It is easy to get overwhelmed while responding to many different competing demands. Further, reunification may occur off-site in an unfamiliar environment. Therefore, staff will maintain control and order and keep accountability for all children. This process is designed to enhance accountability by creating a record and authentication process before the release of each child.

Procedure

Step 1: Establish parent/guardian check-in. Families will check in when they first arrive at the reunification location. They will complete a student information card and provide appropriate identification so that reunification team members may verify their identity. Parents or guardians should be informed that the reunification process is intended to protect both the safety of the child and provide for an accountable transfer of the child from the custody of the school to a recognized custodial parent or guardian.

Step 2: Establish child waiting area. Children will be asked to wait in a separate area until a parent or guardian arrives to pick them up. Children will be engaged by staff in ways that minimize the exposure to the emergency or disaster and imitate a normal day as much as possible. It is not advisable to have parents or guardians go directly to the child waiting area, as the reunification of families may cause other children anxiety, fear, or grief.

Step 3: Establish parent/guardian waiting area. Once families have checked in and identification has been verified, families will be asked to wait in an area while their child is retrieved. A staff member will communicate to the child waiting area via walkie-talkie, runner, or phone, and the child will be brought to the family (Seattle Office of Emergency Management, n.d.).

Specific Considerations for Certain Hazards

Most all-hazards disaster plans include appendices regarding considerations for specific types of disasters. While most skills and tools are useful for all types of hazards, some types of disasters require responses that are specific to that unique situation. By considering differences across specific types of disasters, we can better prepare in the face of any high-priority hazard.

This section summarizes several significant hazards that can happen in communities. Considering these hazards independently allows us to analyze and develop appropriate responses that are tailored to the specific situation. As part of your disaster planning, be sure to analyze what hazards are a threat in your area and focus your energy on augmenting your all-hazards plan to address these specific issues.

Below you will find specific hazards that may impact your community and special considerations that should be addressed in your planning. These considerations go above and beyond your regular all-hazards planning efforts.

Flooding

Flooding is a danger that too many people often ignore, but it is a serious threat to health and safety and can have fatal consequences. More deaths occur each year from flooding than from any other severe weather-related hazard (NWS, n.d.d). Flash floods are flooding events that begin within six hours, and often within three hours, of heavy rainfall leading to high, fast-moving water; flash flooding has occurred in every state in the country. Prolonged flooding from creeks and rivers and flash flooding on roads and from rain-swollen waterways should be addressed as serious threats.

KNOW THE LINGO

- **FLOOD WATCH: flooding or flash flooding is possible**

- **FLOOD WARNING: flooding is occurring or will occur soon and is expected to occur for several days or weeks**

- **FLASH FLOOD WARNING: flash flood is occurring or is imminent**

- **FLOOD ADVISORY: minor flooding of creeks and streams, streets, low-lying areas, or basement flooding is occurring or is imminent**

Tips to Stay Safe and Considerations for Child Care

FEMA offers a free, online flood map website that you can use to determine whether your child-care center or home is located in an area at risk for flooding. Knowing the risk of floods in your area is the first step toward improving your preparedness plan to address this threat. Monitoring NWS and news alerts will allow you to make decisions faster that can keep your staff, the children, and families safe if any type of flooding or flash flooding is possible or imminent.

Many flood-related rescues, injuries, and fatalities result from people in vehicles attempting to drive across flooded roads. Your child-care program needs to consider impacts on transportation during a flooding event. Flooding has the potential to affect the staff's ability to get to work, the parents' ability to drop off or pick up their children, and the program's ability to offer transportation for children, for instance, related to after-school programs.

Keep these tips in mind:

- Use the FEMA website to locate flood maps for your community and child-care center, available here: https://msc.fema.gov/portal/home. Use this information to guide your planning efforts.
- Monitor NWS and news alerts, and rapidly share information with staff and families when appropriate. Develop messages in advance that could be sent out during a flooding event.
- Communicate with families; encourage them to identify two different routes to your program.
- When possible, avoid driving in a flood event, especially with children. When roads are covered with water, you do not know how deep the water is or whether a road has been washed out beneath. Always remember: Turn Around Don't Drown!
- If flooding or flash flooding occurs at the child-care program, have a plan to seek higher ground within the building and know how to get the children upstairs quickly and safely.
- Consider how you would respond to a flooding event. Ensuring drains are clear and free of debris can help. For those located on the first floor, consider obtaining sandbags. These can help reduce the amount of flood-water intrusion into your building.
- Review your emergency and communication plan. When would it become necessary to cancel or shorten programming and activities?
- Flooding can cause other problems. For example, water can be contaminated and can also hide hazards. Ensure you have proper footwear, and avoid flood waters if possible. If flood waters make contact with consumable goods, such as foods or liquids, discard those items.
- Consider adding a sump pump with a battery backup to your facility. Flooding and power outages often occur simultaneously. Having a sump pump with battery backup ensures water will continue to be removed from your facility, even when the power is out.
- Heed the warnings from the NWS. Its Turn Around Don't Drown campaign seeks to educate drivers about the dangers of floods and flooded roads (NWS,

n.d.d). More than half of flood-related drownings occur after a vehicle is driven into flooded streets or roads. If your program offers transportation for children, ensure drivers are aware of the dangers from flooding. Likewise, remind families so they are not tempted to drive through flooded roadways on their way to or from your program. Tips from the NWS include:

> Six inches of water will reach the bottom of most passenger cars, causing loss of control and possible stalling.

> A foot of water will float many vehicles.

> Two feet of rushing water can carry away most vehicles, including sport utility vehicles (SUVs) and pickups.

Earthquakes

Earthquakes occur without warning when there is a sudden release of energy along fault lines in the Earth. There is no reliable system to warn of or predict earthquakes. When experiencing an earthquake, the ground beneath you will shake. Large earthquakes can set off a series of other events with implications for disaster planning, including aftershocks, landslides, and tsunamis.

KNOW THE LINGO

- **EARTHQUAKE OR SEISMIC RISK: the expected or probable impacts (death, injury, building damage) that will happen given the probability of an earthquake occurring in an area**

- **EPICENTER: the site on the Earth's crust directly above the place where the seismic rupture originated**

- **AFTERSHOCK: secondary tremor that can happen after a large earthquake. Tremors from aftershocks can occur over weeks, months, or years.**

- **INTENSITY: a subjective index (or number) to describe the severity of an earthquake in terms of the effect it has on buildings and human life**

Tips to Stay Safe and Considerations for Child Care

FEMA offers earthquake hazard maps that can help you understand the risk of an earthquake in your area. If your child-care program is in an area at risk of earthquakes, take additional steps to prepare specifically for this hazard. Before an earthquake, make sure that your child-care program's structure is physically sound and up to building-code requirements. If it is not, make the appropriate adjustments in advance of a disaster. Additionally, be sure that cabinets, bookcases, microwaves, televisions, and other large furniture and appliance items are anchored and secured to the walls. This prevents them from tipping over when earthquakes occur.

There are several considerations and steps to take immediately following an earthquake. Following guidance and notification with updates, warnings, or instructional messages from local and national authorities is important, as there could be continued threats of fire, unsafe areas, building collapse, aftershocks, or other hazards. Immediately following the earthquake, children and staff may need to be evacuated if your child-care program's structure is damaged and there is a likelihood of more damage through aftershocks. Make plans and partnerships for evacuation in advance. While we shelter in place during an earthquake, evacuation may be possible after the earthquake.

After an earthquake and before you reenter your facility, conduct a structural assessment of your child-care program to determine whether it is safe to continue using the space. If you rent space for your program, these are discussions you should have with your landlord in advance of an event. If several buildings are impacted in your area, it could be an extended period before your child-care program can reopen. Consider your communications plan to share the status of the building with your staff and families, and identify partners who can help you get an assessment completed and/or repairs underway.

Keep these tips in mind:

o Use the FEMA Earthquake Hazard Maps to determine the risk to your community and child-care program, available here: https://www.fema.gov/earthquake-hazard-maps

o If the child-care program's building is structurally damaged, make sure everyone safely evacuates the building immediately. Ensure you have procedures to make sure all staff and children make it out safely.

o Search-and-rescue efforts may be necessary if anyone is trapped in buildings or structures; communicate quickly and clearly with local authorities and make sure they know children are inside. This also highlights the importance of ensuring you have a functional accountability system that allows you and first responders to know exactly how many individuals are present at your program at any given time.

o Assess any structural damage to the child-care program before reentering. This will require working with professional structural engineers. Repairs may be needed before reentry is safe. If renting, discuss this process with your landlord. If you own your building, review your insurance policies to see what types of damages are covered.

o Debris clearance may be necessary to remove and dispose of wreckage and materials if the building is impacted. Having an established list of contractors ahead of time can be useful. After a disaster, we often see inexperienced or unqualified individuals coming into areas to make a quick dollar. These individuals are usually unreliable and quickly vanish once payment is made. It is far better to have a list of local contractors with whom you can establish a relationship and vet before any disasters.

Hurricanes

Hurricanes are severe tropical cyclones with sustained winds above 74 miles per hour. They typically occur along the Gulf of Mexico, the East Coast of the United States, in the Caribbean, or in the Pacific near California, Mexico, or Hawaii. Hurricanes are, on average, three hundred miles across and can be long lasting. The outer rain bands are made up of dense bands of thunderstorms that have tropical-force winds and heavy rains. Tropical-force winds can reach out hundreds of miles from the storm's center (called the *eye*) in a large hurricane (NWS, n.d.a).

The main hazards associated with hurricanes are high, sustained winds; flooding from storm surge; heavy, long-lasting rains; and impacts of heavy waves. If your child-care program is in an area at risk of a hurricane, take a vulnerability assessment and prepare for the highest category of the hurricane that is likely to strike that area.

KNOW THE LINGO

- **HURRICANE CATEGORIES: The destructive force of a hurricane is categorized using the Saffir-Simpson scale, with categories ranging from 1 to 5. Wind speed, storm surge, and waves contribute toward category levels, with Category 1 indicating a wind speed of 74–95 miles per hour and a Category 5 indicating wind speeds of 156 miles or higher per hour.**

- **STORM SURGE: Ocean water is pushed toward shore by the hurricane's winds and combines with the normal tide; water levels can reach 30 feet or more and can cause severe flooding (NOAA, 2019).**

- **EYE: calm center of the hurricane, surrounded by the eyewall, which has the heaviest rain and strongest surface winds of the storm**

(University of Rhode Island, 2015)

Tips to Stay Safe and Considerations for Child Care

Hurricanes are disasters with notice. Typically, there are warnings a few days in advance that allow you time to prepare. It is extremely important to listen to guidance from local authorities. If it is recommended or required that you evacuate your area, then you should have a plan in place. Know where to evacuate to, how to communicate to families, and when to close your child-care program. After a hurricane, it could be up to seventy-two hours before help is on the way, so you should consider in advance what supplies are needed. If you are located in a hurricane-prone area, maintain a supply of sandbags, plywood, screws, tarps, and other items that could be used to help lessen the impact of wind and rain. These supplies quickly vanish from stores when a hurricane is approaching, so acquiring them ahead of time will provide you with more time to prepare. Further, a generator can be very helpful in the aftermath of a hurricane. Sadly, we see a lot of deaths due to carbon monoxide poisoning after hurricanes as many individuals will run a generator inside a closed space, such as a garage, or even bring the generator inside so it is less likely to be stolen. Generators produce carbon monoxide gas. Carbon monoxide can't be seen or smelled, but it can quickly kill. Never use a generator indoors. It is also wise to have a battery-operated carbon monoxide detector inside the building to be sure that this deadly gas is not entering the structure.

When a hurricane strikes, power outages, floodwaters, storm surge, or compromised water supply due to flooding may follow. Be prepared for a hurricane to be a long-duration disaster event with lasting impacts.

Keep these tips in mind:

- Determine whether your child-care program is in a location at risk of a hurricane. If so, prepare for the highest potential category hurricane in advance.
- Become familiar with local evacuation routes.
- If a hurricane is likely to form, secure supplies and gas immediately. Do not wait, as gas and supplies often run out.
- Use the fact that you know a hurricane is coming before it arrives to your advantage. In the days and hours leading up to the event, you have ample time to evacuate, communicate with others, get any additional supplies, and be prepared.
- Hurricanes are long-duration events, and you should be prepared to be on your own for seventy-two hours before help is on the way. Ideally, you would have time to inform families that your facility is closed, so no children will be on-site when the hurricane hits.
- Advance notice also gives you an opportunity to board up windows and to secure furniture, toys, and playground equipment that may become airborne during a high-wind event.

Tornadoes

A tornado is a violently rotating column of air extending from a thunderstorm to the ground. The most violent tornadoes are capable of tremendous destruction with wind speeds of 250 miles per hour or more. Damage paths can be more than one mile wide and fifty miles long. Although violent tornadoes comprise only 2 percent of all tornadoes, they are responsible for nearly 70 percent of tornado-related fatalities (National Disaster Education Coalition, 1999).

Tornadoes have been reported in every state; however, in the United States they most frequently occur east of the Rocky Mountains during the spring and summer months. The peak of the tornado season is April through June (NWS, n.d.c). Nationally, twelve hundred tornadoes are reported yearly (National Severe Storms Laboratory, n.d). These tornadoes result in eighty deaths and more than 1,500 injuries. Scientists do not completely understand how tornadoes form; however, we do know that they form from supercell thunderstorms, which contain updrafts that can have winds in excess of 100 miles per hour. Most tornadoes usually last for a few minutes, but in some cases they have lasted for more than an hour.

KNOW THE LINGO

- **BEST AVAILABLE REFUGE AREAS:** areas in a building that have been deemed by a qualified architect or engineer to likely offer the greatest safety for building occupants during a tornado. While these areas do not guarantee safety in a tornado, people using these areas are less likely to be injured or killed than in other areas of a building. See https://www.fema.gov/media-library-data/20130726-1456-20490-4099/fema_p_431.pdf

- **TORNADO WATCH:** issued by the NWS when conditions are favorable for the development of tornadoes in and close to the watch area. The size of the watch area can vary depending on the weather situation.

- **TORNADO WARNING:** issued by the NWS when a tornado is indicated by radar or sighted by spotters. People in the affected area should seek safe shelter immediately. Warnings can be issued without a tornado watch being already in effect.

- **FUJITA SCALE (F-SCALE):** how the intensity of tornadoes is measured:

    » F0: 40 to 72 mph winds—Generally light damage, most frequent type (40 percent)

> » F1: 73 to 112 mph winds—Moderate damage and
> roof lifting, second most frequent (35 percent)
>
> » F2: 113 to 157 mph winds—Significant damage
> with roofs torn off; 20 percent of all tornadoes
>
> » F3: 158 to 207 mph winds—Severe damage to
> homes and trees uprooted
>
> » F4: 208 to 260 mph winds—Devastating damage
> leveling homes; approximately 1 percent of all
> tornadoes
>
> » F5: 261 to 318 mph winds—Incredible damage
> with near total destruction
>
> (Storm Prediction Center, 2020)

Tips to Stay Safe and Considerations for Child Care

First, identify the risk level of experiencing a tornado in your area. Tornadoes are most likely to occur mid-afternoon between 4 and 9 p.m., with early-morning or late-evening tornadoes being much rarer (National Severe Storms Laboratory, n.d.). This means that tornadoes may occur when children are being picked up from your program.

The effects of high winds are an important consideration when determining where to stay during a tornado. If your area is at risk, then identify the best available refuge areas in your building that could hold your staff and children in the event of a tornado. In general, lower-level floors, interior rooms without windows, and areas with minimal amounts of glass, reinforced walls, strong connections between walls and roofs, and short roof spans are advantageous over other types of structures. Hazardous elements within buildings to be aware of include long-span roofs, lightweight roofs, heavier roofs, windows, unprotected corridors, and masonry walls.

Also, identify a predetermined location where you could go with your staff and children in the event of notice that a tornado may be on the way. As part of this process, consider what items you would need to bring with you, depending on the age of the children in your program's care. Typically, early childhood programs that experience tornadoes develop a go-bag or tornado kit that includes toys, games, stuffed animals, snacks, diapers, hand wipes, food, water, flashlights, a weather or AM/FM radio, and any necessary medicine. Tornado watches and warnings can be long-duration events, so be sure ensure your supplies will last for at least one hour.

While there is often limited notice of a tornado, having a NOAA battery-operated weather radio can ensure that you receive timely updates and information as soon as they become available.

Keep these tips in mind:

- Determine your child-care program's risk of experiencing a tornado, and plan accordingly.
- Use a NOAA weather radio to ensure your program receives any watches or warnings of a tornado on the way. Using NOAA's Specific Area Message Encoder (SAME) technology, you can receive alerts specific to your location.
- Consider the best available refuge area within your building and a predetermined location to move to if time allows. A best available refuge may not guarantee full safety, depending on how the facility was built, but it should be the safest location available within the facility.
- These situations can be scary, but it is our job as early childhood professionals to ensure we are projecting calm to the children. Some programs have developed special games or songs to sing during these events. Others have created tornado shirts, which children put on during threats from severe weather. The shirts contain vital information about the child—age, phone number, parents' or guardians' names, address, allergies—so that children can be quickly identified if they get separated. However, early childhood providers do not share the true purpose of these shirts with the children. Instead, they make it into a fun game for children and treat the event like a fashion show or game of dress-up.
- Once you have identified your area of refuge, conduct practice drills so that children and staff become familiar with the area and the routes to access it.
- Your staff and children may be together in a tight space for an extended period waiting for the storm to pass. Make sure you have necessary age-appropriate items as well as items to keep the children occupied.

Chemical Spills and Hazardous Materials

A *hazardous material* is defined as any type of matter (solid, liquid, or gas) or energy that is capable of imposing harm when released to people, the environment, and property, including weapons of mass destruction. Chemical manufacturers, distributors, and vendors are typical sources of hazardous materials, as are hazardous-material waste sites and users, such as service stations, manufacturing facilities, and hospitals.

Chemical spills or releases can happen during production, storage, transportation, use, or disposal. Fixed facilities, such as an industrial plant, are the most likely place for a hazardous incident to occur. Other more common areas include railroads, highways, pipelines, and waterways. Homes, schools, and businesses situated near the site of a hazardous-materials spill or release are at most risk if the material is airborne, contaminates a nearby water source, or poses any threat outside of the accident site.

- **US DEPARTMENT OF TRANSPORTATION (DOT) HAZARD CLASSIFICATION SYSTEM:** the hazard class of dangerous goods is indicated by either its class number or name:

  » Class 1: Explosives

  » Class 2: Gases

  » Class 3: Flammable liquids (and combustible liquids)

  » Class 4: Flammable solids, substances liable to spontaneously combust, substances that emit flammable gases on contact with water

  » Class 5: Oxidizing substances and organic peroxides

  » Class 6: Toxic (poisonous) substances

  » Class 7: Radioactive materials

  » Class 8: Corrosive substances

  » Class 9: Miscellaneous dangerous goods/ hazardous materials and articles (US DOT, 2018)

- **THERMAL HARM:** external or internal injuries caused by exposure to temperature extremes from contacting a fire or other heat source, frostbite from low-temperature materials, or inhaling fumes/heated air

- **RADIOLOGICAL HARM:** injury caused by exposure to radiation. Perhaps the most dangerous since the most harmful types of radiation cannot be seen, smelled, or felt. Ionizing radiation is the type that poses a threat to humans and causes damage to living cells and DNA. Children are especially impacted by radiation due to their smaller bodies and less-developed immune systems.

- **ASPHYXIATION:** suffocation caused by exposure to materials that reduce oxygen levels in the surrounding atmosphere. A person exposed to the material cannot get enough oxygen through the lungs, and the person slowly suffocates. Many asphyxiants are odorless and tasteless, thus you or the children may become unconscious without realizing a gas is present.

- **CHEMICAL HARM:** various illnesses caused by exposure to chemicals, such as poisons and corrosives. The degree of impact varies depending on the material.

- **ETIOLOGICAL (BIOLOGICAL) HARM:** pathogenic illnesses caused by exposure to biological materials, such as bacteria, viruses, and biological toxins. Symptoms are often delayed since pathogens take time to multiply and develop a significant foundation.

- **MECHANICAL HARM:** injury or death, such as initial injury from fragmentation or flying debris, blast overpressure (rapid increase in air pressure, which harms a person internally), or secondary blast injuries (when a person is thrown into other objects). This results from exposure to or contact with fragmentation or debris due to a pressure release, explosion, or boiling liquid expanding vapor explosion (BLEVE). The degree of harm is based on the size of the incident and the person's proximity to the incident.

- **PERSONAL PROTECTIVE EQUIPMENT (PPE):** essential protective gear, including respirators, eye protection, hearing protection, and protective clothing, are the main barrier between you and the hazard. Recommendations for PPE will change depending on the situation at hand. Make sure to listen to first responders, and ensure staff and children have access to proper PPE.

Tips to Stay Safe and Considerations for Child Care

In the event of a chemical spill or exposure to hazardous materials, first responders will use a risk-based response process to assess the incident and determine the threat to localities, such as your child-care facility. First responders will use tools such as the Emergency Response Guidebook issued by the DOT to aid in quick identification of the hazardous material, ensure the health of responders and the nearby public during mitigation, determine a plan to improve the situation, and implement the planned response actions. Your staff should be able to be reached at all times to stay updated on the response plans so that your facility may act accordingly and avoid any exposure to the hazardous environment.

Your child-care facility must plan emergency responses to possible hazardous-material instances. You can gather information to help you plan your responses from your Local Emergency Planning Committee (LEPC), FEMA, the American Red Cross, and the Environmental Protection Agency (EPA). Learn about your community and federal emergency plans to gauge what responses would fit best for your facility. General emergency packs, with first-aid supplies, water, snacks, and batteries, should be available to all classrooms.

It is most important to adhere to instructions from first responders. Action plans should be set in motion according to the guidance of authorities after they have assessed the situation to ensure proper safety for staff and children. Constantly listen to local radio and television for information.

Basic steps your staff and the children can take to maximize safety are as follows:

o Stay away from the incident area to minimize the risk of contamination.
o Be ready to evacuate, shelter in place, or lockdown rapidly if instructed.
o If you are outside, ensure all individuals are upstream, uphill, and upwind of the hazardous substance.
o If you are instructed to stay indoors, select rooms above ground, seal the room, and leave approximately 10 square feet between persons to prevent carbon dioxide buildup.

Power Outages

A *power outage* is the unexpected loss of electrical power networks, which may result in disrupted communications, water, and transportation causing schools, businesses, and other services to close. Other complications include spoilage of food, water contamination, and faults with medical devices.

KNOW THE LINGO

- **POWER GRID: interconnected network of electrical transmission lines used to deliver electricity from numerous producers to consumers over a wide area**

- **HIGH VOLTAGE: an electrical potential large enough to cause injury or damage, typically over 600 volts**

- **SURGE PROTECTOR: protects electronics from power surges in the electrical system, which could spark a fire or electrocute a person**

Tips to Stay Safe and Considerations for Child Care

Approximately 44 percent of power outages are caused by storms (FEMA, n.d.b). Some preparedness experts estimate that nearly 70 percent of US businesses will be affected by a power outage in the next year (FEMA, n.d.b). Even during severe events, report any outages to your power company. First, they may not be aware of the outage in your area. Second, when you report the outage, indicate you are caring for children, which may place you higher up on the restoration priority list. To better prepare, install emergency lighting, have flashlights and extra batteries handy, and be sure that emergency lighting on exit signs is operational.

Keep these tips in mind:

- Keep freezers and refrigerators closed; food in the refrigerator will last approximately four hours, the freezer may last longer.
- To avoid carbon monoxide poisoning, only use generators outside and away from windows.
- Never use a gas stove to provide heat.
- Disconnect all appliances and electronics that use electricity.
- If a prolonged outage occurs during extreme hot or cold weather, consider relocating to an alternate location for heat and cooling.
- Use surge protectors.
- Keep extra batteries and flashlights on hand.

Food Safety

Food safety is the process of ensuring that food is stored properly and is safe to consume. Food safety is extremely important in various disasters, especially during floods or disasters that result in power outages.

KNOW THE LINGO

- **POTENTIALLY HAZARDOUS FOODS: foods that were in a refrigerator or freezer when the power went out but have been thawed and/or are warmer than 40 degrees F. Foods to be concerned about after a power outage include meat, fish, poultry, dairy, eggs, soft cheeses, cooked beans, rice, potatoes, pasta, and so on.**

- **SAFE FOODS: carbonated beverages; unopened, nonperishable foods**

Tips to Stay Safe and Considerations for Child Care

In the event of a disaster, food may become compromised, and early childhood professionals should understand food-safety principles to stay safe. Maintaining temperatures is vital for food safety. If, for example, the power is out causing the freezer to turn off and frozen food becomes warmer than 40 degrees Fahrenheit, it is at an unsafe temperature, meaning that any bacteria present before freezing can begin to multiply (Office of Disease Prevention and Health Promotion, 2020). Further, food that has come into contact with flood waters may be contaminated and should be thrown away (Foodsafety.gov, 2019). Food represents a large portion of expenditures in the early childhood setting, so some programs may be hesitant to discard spoiled or suspect food. In these cases, the costs of getting a child or staff member sick far outweigh the benefits. Policies should err on the side of food safety rather than cost savings. This may be an area to discuss with your insurance carrier, as some do provide reimbursement if food is lost or unusable because of an emergency or disaster.

6

Testing and Revising Your Emergency Plan

Creating an emergency plan is a vital part of the preparedness process. Once the plan is complete, test the plan. This allows staff members to become more familiar with the plan's contents and also helps to identify any areas that may be problematic or not reality based.

Many jurisdictions require a complete review and revision of emergency plans each year. While this requirement can be helpful, if we only review our plan once a year, we are missing the purpose of conducting drills and exercises.

The plan should be reviewed every time your program conducts an emergency drill. Before the drill, staff members should review the plan and refresh their memories of their assigned tasks and overall objectives. During the drill, staff should carry out the policies and procedures documented in the plan. After the drill, staff should discuss whether or not the plan accounted for real-world factors. You should also review the plan and possibly update it in the following circumstances:

- When your program has changed its operating hours
- When you have changed the ages of children served or the licensed capacity (number of children served)
- With changes in staffing, whether adding new staff or decreasing the overall number of staff
- When you have made changes to the building layout, design, or flow
- With changes in the surrounding area that affect your program, such as new traffic patterns, new neighbors, a change in risk factors, new infrastructure, and so on
- With new licensure requirements

The most effective emergency plans are those that are consistently reviewed, exercised, and updated. Your emergency plan should be a living and breathing document, not a document that sits idle on a shelf. Too often, plans fail because no one is aware of their existence and the plans have not been routinely tested. Each staff member should be aware of and able to execute the plan.

The Importance of Exercises

Ensuring that your staff is familiar with your emergency-preparedness plan and that the plan operates successfully under real-world conditions are of paramount importance. One simple way to test your plan is to use it as your action guide when conducting drills and exercises. The plan should be the main source of information used to inform actions and decisions during exercises, drills, and real-world emergencies.

As the likelihood of an emergency is low, exercises and drills are the primary way to test assumptions, identify areas for improvement, and highlight any gaps that may exist. The purpose of creating an emergency plan is to think about, decide, and commit to a series of actions ahead of time. This allows you to draw on your knowledge, experience, and training during an emergency. You do not want to be developing your emergency plan during the emergency. Rather, you want to draw from the knowledge gained from your emergency planning and exercising process so that your actions are well thought out, identified, and tested.

Required Drills

Required monthly drills should be conducted in a meaningful way. Too often, monthly fire drills are not taken seriously or the fire drill is conducted the same way each month. Drills are meant to test our responses, actions, and plans. If we always make a left out of the classroom, go down the hallway, make a right, and exit the building, then we are missing the point of the drills. Instead, drills should be used to test different approaches and responses.

For example, if your normal plan is to go out of the classroom and turn left, then during the next fire drill, pretend that the fire is located outside of the classroom on the left. This inserts an element of surprise into the exercise and breaks up the mundane approach. Further, this allows staff to make on-the-fly decisions like those that they will be expected to make in the event of a real emergency. After all, emergencies rarely play out the way we have planned.

Pull together your staff or visit each staff member individually once the drill has concluded. Discuss their decision-making processes and how the changed conditions affected their typical responses. Ask about how the new plan worked. Were there any challenges? any new considerations? any issues that were identified that need to be incorporated into a revision of the plan?

Tabletop and Cognitive Exercises

Not every drill needs to involve physical movement or even the participation of children. You can also engage your staff members by conducting tabletop and/or cognitive exercises that relate to emergency preparedness. Perform these on routine days or during staff retreats. A tabletop exercise is an activity designed to test your emergency-preparedness planning and assumptions. It is a cognitive exercise in which you provide a scenario and staff talk through the various emergency-response options and policy considerations that would be relevant. This approach is helpful in staff training as well as in emergency plan development and revision.

At the beginning of the day, approach your staff and tell them that you would like for them to think about a scenario that you give them. They will be given the balance of the morning to think about the scenario. Then, at lunch, ask them how they would handle the situation. The scenario can be simple or complex, depending on the amount of time available for discussion. Open-ended questions are best because they allow the staff to think about their responses and identify potential issues or barriers. Take a look at the following examples:

> I am sure you have seen the construction down the street. This morning I would like you to spend a bit of time thinking about what we would do if the construction crew accidentally hit a gas line, and we suddenly had to evacuate our program. I am going to check back in with you at lunch, and I would like for you to tell me your ideas about how we would evacuate your classroom, how we would communicate with families, and where we would take the children. Encourage your staff to also think about what support they would need during and after the event and what they would do if the director were absent.

> We have been notified that there is ongoing criminal activity in the area. We have moved all of the children inside and have suspended outdoor playtime. Law enforcement has informed us that this is an ongoing situation that could last several hours. Pickup time is an hour away. Roads are closed around our facility due to the criminal activity. No one should be allowed in or out of our building, per law enforcement guidance. What should our top priorities be? How should we handle the children? What and how should we communicate with families?

Conclusion

Being prepared for emergencies and disasters is an ongoing commitment. Many factors necessitate the need to reevaluate and update our emergency plans. Changes to staffing, building design, governing regulations, or the emergence of new threats all require the review and reevaluation of our emergency plans.

Much like other required tasks, emergency-preparedness planning often falls to the bottom of the priority list, with organizations doing little more than checking the box to ensure compliance. Taking this approach with preparedness means that you miss opportunities for improvement. When done properly, preparedness efforts allow us to bolster staff confidence, empower staff, educate children, and increase parental confidence in our programs. Further, the emergency-preparedness environment is ripe with learning opportunities to support science, technology, reading, engineering, arts, and mathematics (STREAM) education to the children in our care. We can use our disaster drills as an opportunity to educate children on why disasters happen. In turn, this can help ease their anxieties and engage them in our preparedness process. Supplies, such as a solar-powered cell phone charger, can be used, for example, to demonstrate to children how the sun can be turned into electricity.

In the aftermath of a disaster, we can also use STREAM to show how our natural environment recovers. After the devasting hurricane in Puerto Rico, teachers had to get creative, as many did not have power for nearly nine months. Teachers embraced STREAM and worked with children to create lessons that explored the outside world. Much of the vegetation had been destroyed by the hurricane; STREAM principles allowed teachers to show how living organisms rebuild and regrow—just like humans do. You can build on the natural connection between STREAM and emergency preparedness to support learning. As many STREAM projects utilize common classroom items, early childhood teachers can develop meaningful lesson plans that help children cope with disasters while also learning more about the environment around them (Roszak, 2019). Likewise, preparedness offers us a tremendous opportunity to further engage with our community and develop valuable networks with community members, social-service providers, and first-responder organizations.

Overall, our shared goal is to ensure our programs are as safe as they can possibly be for the children and families we serve and for our staff members. I appreciate the time that you have invested reading this book, and hope that you have found the information helpful in advancing your knowledge on this topic. Remember, preparedness does save lives. The more we can plan, exercise, and prepare ahead of time, the better the results will be when we are faced with an emergency or disaster. In the next chapter, we look at sample emergency plans to help you develop, update, and practice the plans for your center.

Don't be scared. Be prepared.™

7

Sample Emergency Plans

Developing, updating, and practicing use of your emergency plan is vital. Use the templates in this chapter as a starting point for developing or updating your emergency plan. Make the plan relevant and useful to your geographic region and child-care program. Share these plans with key community stakeholders and adjust as needed. Customize these samples based on your local rules, regulations, and requirements.

Policy on Fire Drills

Purpose: These required monthly drills provide an opportunity for staff and children to practice our response to a fire.

Procedure: The director has discretion as to whether staff will be notified in advance of the fire drill. Generally, staff will be notified in advance at the beginning of the school year. This advance notice will give staff time beforehand to discuss the drill with children and ensure they have been briefed on their role and expected behavior. This also provides an opportunity for children to ask questions and makes the event less scary for children.

Drills must be conducted once a month. Drills will be conducted on different days and at different times each month. At least twice a year, the director will ask that staff and children use the secondary and tertiary (if available) exits. This allows staff and children an opportunity to think about the various exit paths from the classrooms. The director may also erect a "burning bush," which is a tree made out of paper that simulates a fire. In the event the burning bush is in the path of your primary evacuation route, you should consider the path blocked and attempt to evacuate through another exit.

In the event the secondary or tertiary exit is a window, staff will go to the window and ensure the window can be fully opened enough so that children and staff could escape through the window. Once the teacher has opened the window, she will then close the window and evacuate the children through the primary exit.

We will not actually be using the window to escape during the drill. However, this option allows us to ensure that the windows are fully functioning and unobstructed.

Steps when Conducting a Fire Drill

1. When the alarm goes off, staff are to evacuate the building. The staff will take the emergency backpack and evacuate the children out of the building following the posted evacuation route. Children (infants) who are not walking should be placed in an evacuation crib (not to exceed four to a crib), and the crib should be wheeled outside to the designated area. Toddlers (walkers) proceed immediately with staff to the outside designated area.

    The lead teachers for each classroom shall:

    o Check each exit door for proper functioning.
    o Ensure all exit and emergency lighting is properly functioning.
    o Examine all exit pathways and make sure they are clear and free from debris.
    o Ensure all evacuation maps are clearly posted and current.
    o Review the contents of all emergency go-bags.

2. Each staff member shall take attendance and determine the presence of each child currently in attendance. This can be done using the class lists in each emergency backpack.

3. The director or business manager is responsible for checking the whole building (including bathrooms) and ensuring all staff have evacuated the building.

4. After all staff and children have been accounted for, the director or designee shall notify everyone to return to the building.

5. The director or designee is responsible for documenting the fire drill on the fire-drill log. This log includes the number of children and staff present, the date and time, the weather conditions, and the time it took to conduct the drill.

6. After the drill is over, the classroom teachers should take a moment and ensure all emergency equipment is present and functioning properly. This includes flashlights, radios, and so on. Any missing or inoperable items should be reported to the director.

Policy on Emergency Response to a Fire

Purpose: These procedures are intended to ensure that staff and children are prepared and know how to respond to a fire.

Procedure: Staff should be familiar with the evacuation procedure, including the locations of exits, fire/smoke detectors, and fire extinguishers.

Steps for Emergency Response to a Fire

1. If a fire/smoke is discovered, immediately activate the nearest pull station and/or call 911. Notify the other adults via the walkie-talkies or through verbal communication.

2. If the fire is small (wastepaper-basket size) and you are comfortable doing so, extinguish the fire by using a fire extinguisher.

3. DO NOT TAKE RISKS. Personal safety and the safety of the children come first.

4. If the fire is larger, or if the smoke makes it difficult to determine the fire location, evacuate the area and report to the designated evacuation area.

5. Leave personal belongings behind. This may include evacuating children without shoes or coats. If possible, bring the emergency backpack with you as you leave the building.

6. When exiting a room, use the back of the hands to touch the door, doorknob, and door frame. If any are hot, do not open the door.

7. When exiting the building, be aware of the wind direction and avoid the smoke as much as possible.

8. Follow the procedures practiced during monthly fire drills. Be prepared to use primary, secondary, or tertiary exits if necessary. Move the children quickly to safety. Proceed to the designated evacuation point.

9. Once outside and a safe distance away from the building, take attendance.

10. Report your whereabouts and attendance to the director or business manager.

11. Stay out of the building until advised by the director or the fire department that it is safe to return.

Policy on Evacuation

Purpose: The safety of our staff, children, families, and visitors are of the utmost importance to us. During an emergency or disaster situation that compromises the structural integrity of the building, or if staying in the building could cause unnecessary threat or harm, then we will evacuate the building. Our primary purpose is to reduce the possibility of injury or harm.

Procedure: A decision to evacuate should be made after weighing the risk of staying in the building against the potential harms and threats of evacuating. Our default position is to stay in the building, but in the event that the risks of staying inside outweigh the benefits of leaving, then an evacuation is appropriate. Examples of threats that could cause evacuations include a chemical spill, structural damage, a bomb threat, an act of violence, fire, and prolonged utility outage, among others.

Chain of Command

The director or business manager shall determine whether an evacuation is needed.

Once an evacuation has been ordered, the director shall assume command and control of the situation. If the director is unavailable, then the business manager shall assume the duties assigned to the director. If both the director and business manager are unavailable, then the lead teacher with the most seniority shall assume command and control.

Responsibilities of the Person in Charge

1. Ensure that 911 has been notified, if applicable.
2. Taking into account the situation, if possible and safe to do so, inspect all closets and bathrooms to ensure that the building has been completely vacated. Given the nature of the emergency, this may or may not be possible. Remember that safety is of the utmost importance.
3. Receive attendance reports from all classrooms.
4. Communicate and serve as the primary point of contact with responding emergency services. They may request building information, such as entrances and exits and the overall layout of the building. They may also request occupant information, such as the number of individuals in the building and their respective ages. Report any missing or unaccounted for individuals to emergency services.
5. If necessary, coordinate the reunification efforts. Identify a safe area where all personnel and children can reunify. Choose a location that is far enough away from the incident to be safe (ideally, one of the existing identified evacuation locations). Also be mindful of the need for shelter, especially in case of inclement weather. Communicate this plan using the walkie-talkie or mobile texting. Once this is accomplished, follow your reunification plan.
6. Once the situation is deemed over or stabilized, determine whether early dismissal is appropriate or if it is safe to return to normal programming at the facility.
7. Determine the appropriate communication strategy. This may require communicating with families and parents, licensing, and other community officials.

Responsibilities of Staff

1. Once a determination has been made that evacuation is needed, the appropriate information shall be communicated to all members of the staff. Communication will occur using the fastest means available. This may include phone, radio, intercom, or direct contact.
2. Once the initial evacuation order has been communicated, staff will keep in touch via the walkie-talkies, which should be turned on and set to channel #3. In the event the walkie-talkies do not work or are inaccessible, staff should use mobile texting as a backup.

3. During the evacuation, staff should keep radio traffic on the walkie-talkies to a minimum and only communicate important or time-sensitive information.

4. Upon receiving notification of an evacuation, each classroom will move calmly and swiftly with the children assigned to the classroom to the nearest exit. If the primary exit is unusable or unreachable, proceed to the secondary or tertiary exit.

5. If necessary, evacuation cribs may be used for infants and young toddlers. No more than four children shall be placed in any one evacuation crib.

6. Depending on the type of emergency necessitating the evacuation, there may or may not be time to obtain coats, shoes, or other personal belongings. In any event, limit the number of items to be carried, as it will be beneficial to have free hands. For those situations requiring immediate evacuation, leave all personal belongings behind, including coats, shoes, and so on.

7. Each classroom shall take the emergency go-bag with them as they exit, so long as doing so does not unnecessarily prolong or hinder the evacuation process.

8. If windows are used as an evacuation route, an adult will go out the window first and then provide assistance as the children are placed out of the window. One adult will stay in the room until all children are successfully evacuated.

9. Proceed to the primary evacuation area. If the primary area is unsafe or unreachable, then proceed to the secondary evacuation area.

10. Upon arrival at the evacuation area, take attendance immediately. Communicate the attendance information, along with the arrival to the evacuation area, to the person in charge.

11. Await further instructions from the person in charge about how to proceed. Decisions regarding relocation, family reunification, implementation of an early pickup, or whether it is safe to return to the building and resume operations will be made by the person in charge.

Responsibilities of All Occupants, Including Staff, Parents, and Visitors

1. Be familiar with the locations of all exits.

2. Follow and cooperate with staff directions.

3. Provide assistance as requested by staff members.

4. Once you have exited the building, you are not to return inside.

Policy on Lockdown

Purpose: A lockdown will be used when there is a risk of hostile activity. The goal of a lockdown is to create a secure location that serves as a safe barrier from the threat. The lockdown should also serve to raise the awareness levels of all the adults in the building; we need them to be our eyes and ears during this time. Our efforts are aimed at physically preventing the threat from entering our space.

Procedure: The decision to implement lockdown procedures should be made upon assessing the threat an individual may pose to children and staff. The most common reason for implementing a lockdown is due to an unauthorized individual or intruder on-site. Lockdowns may also occur in coordination with local law enforcement, if there is a notable threat in the vicinity of the program such as a violent criminal at large.

Chain of Command

The director or business manager shall determine if a lockdown is needed.

Once a lockdown has been ordered, the director shall assume command and control of the situation. If the director is unavailable, then the business manager shall assume the duties assigned to the director. If both the director and business manager are unavailable, then the lead teacher with the most seniority shall assume command and control.

Responsibilities of the Person in Charge

1. Ensure that 911 has been notified, if applicable. If alerted by local authorities, maintain communication while the threat is ongoing.
2. Once the situation is deemed over or stabilized, determine whether early dismissal is appropriate or if it is safe to return to normal programming at the facility.
3. Determine the appropriate communication strategy. This may require communicating with families and parents, licensing, and community officials.
4. During a lockdown, individuals will not be allowed in or out of the program areas. Keep this in mind when communicating with families, as parents and guardians will not be allowed to retrieve their children while the lockdown is in effect. Further, the neighborhood may be inaccessible due to law enforcement barricades, checkpoints, or closures. If communicating with families, it will be important to have them remain where they are until the lockdown is over.
5. Ensure all staff are aware of the lockdown and that outdoor activities are suspended until further notice.

Responsibilities of Staff

1. Keep calm and take measures so as not to frighten the children.
2. Move away from windows. If the windows are equipped with blinds or other covering devices, use them to cover the windows.
3. Ensure all external doors are locked. Depending on the situation, you may be asked to barricade the doors.
4. Ensure all staff are aware of the lockdown and that outdoor activities are suspended until further notice.

5. Move to an interior portion of the building, ideally in a location that does not have windows.
6. Keep children safe, calm, and quiet until the lockdown is over. Attempt to make this a normal day by engaging them in quiet games or softly reading books to them.

Policy on Disgruntled or Impaired Visitors and Violent Acts

Purpose: This policy covers impaired or disgruntled visitors and acts of violence or hostile intruders, including active shooters. The safety of our staff and the children trusted to our care is of the utmost importance to us.

Procedure: Visitors and guests are welcome at our program. However, our preference is to preschedule visitors and tours so that we may provide adequate notice and ensure staff coverage. Our number one priority is the safety of the children entrusted in our care and to our staff. Therefore, all employees are empowered to deny entry to a visitor or guest, if they feel that doing so would be in the best interest of the safety of our facility.

For those guests and visitors who are allowed entry, all reasonable precautions must be taken, including the following:

- Visitors and guests should ring the bell/intercom and request entry into our program. The staff person answering this bell/intercom shall ascertain the individual's identity and purpose for requesting entry into our facility.
- Visitors and guests are required to sign in and out at the front-desk area. Our policy is to also make a copy of the visitor's or guest's driver's license.
- Once granted entry, visitors or guests will be provided with a sticker/badge that identifies them as visitors.
- All visitors must be escorted by a staff member while on the property. Visitors should never be left unattended in areas with children.
- When visitors or guests are leaving the facility, they are to sign out and return the visitor/guest badges.

Responsibilities of Staff

As staff members, each of us has a responsibility to ensure our safety policies and procedures are followed. Each staff member shall:

- Ensure all exterior doors are marked with a notice instructing visitors to go to the main entrance.
- Ensure the main entrance contains signage that directs all guests and visitors to immediately report to the office.
- Ensure all exterior doors are locked throughout the workday, to prevent unauthorized access from the outside into our secured program space.
- Understand that they are empowered. Staff members are expected to question unfamiliar faces, especially those who are not with an escort. Staff

members should introduce themselves, attempt to elicit the guest's name, and ask "May I help you?"

o Provide advance notice to the front office of any guests or visitors who will be visiting.

o Ensure authorized guests or visitors are escorted during the duration of their visit.

Disgruntled or Impaired Visitors or Guests

If any staff member, at anytime, has reason to believe that any person picking up a child or interacting with a child is under the influence of alcohol or drugs or is physically or emotionally impaired in any way that may endanger a child, the staff member should contact the director. If the director is not available, the staff member should contact the business manager. The safety of our staff and of the children in our care is our top priority.

If the individual is outside the building:

o Staff shall utilize the door entry system to first determine who does and does not belong in our space. Visitors are required to state their name and purpose of visit. All visitors are required to be manually buzzed into the building.

o If a visitor is unknown, appears agitated, or in the judgment of the individual answering the buzzer, appears hostile, the visitor should be refused entry to the building.

o The staff member should immediately call 911. If unable to call 911, attempt to communicate with other staff members about the potential problem and have them call 911 from a location out of earshot of the individual in question.

o Staff members caring for children should be ready to evacuate the building or implement lockdown procedures.

o If possible, move the child of the individual (in the case of a parent or guardian) to another classroom or location out of view.

If the individual is already in the building:

o Staff should attempt to isolate the potential aggressor from as many adults and children as possible. Seek to draw the individual to the office or another less-populated space.

o Never put the potential aggressor between yourself and an exit. You always want the ability to exit the room if the need arises.

o The staff member should immediately call 911. If unable to call 911, attempt to communicate with other staff members about the potential problem and have them call 911 from a location out of earshot of the individual in question.

o Staff members caring for children should be ready to evacuate the building or implement lockdown procedures.

o If possible, move the child of the individual (in the case of a parent or guardian) to another classroom or location out of view.

If the individual has entered a classroom:

- Staff should attempt to draw the individual into an area that is not populated with children. Other staff members should attempt to remove children from the classroom and away from the situation.
- If comfortable doing so, engage the potential aggressor in agreeable conversation to deescalate the situation. Remain calm and be polite. Use words that express empathy and understanding.
- Attempt to engage or stall the individual until help can arrive.
- Staff who are out of earshot of the individual should immediately call 911. If unable to call 911, attempt to communicate with other staff members about the potential problem and have them call 911 from a location out of earshot of the individual in question.
- Staff members caring for children should be ready to evacuate the building or implement lockdown procedures.
- When law enforcement arrives, turn the situation over to them.

After the incident, or as soon as it is reasonable to do so, conduct an after action-review of the situation with staff.

Change any locks or door codes that may have been compromised in this incident.

Active Shooter

During an active-shooter incident, staff members are expected to follow the procedures as outlined and any verbal instructions from site management, law enforcement, or other emergency personnel.

Act in a professional manner. All staff are empowered to make decisions. This policy provides general information and action guidance; however, active-shooter situations are fluid and no plan can cover every situation. Staff are required to become familiar with this policy and apply the themes, techniques, tactics, and guidance as appropriate during an emergency. This will require exercise of professional judgment by the staff members.

- **Call 911:** All staff have the authority to call 911, and a call to 911 is of the highest importance. When calling 911, provide as much information as possible, including our program name, street address, and the fact that we have children at this location. If staff is able, provide the location of the shooter, as well as a description of the person(s) with the weapon and the type of weapon. If safe to do so, stay on the line to relay information. Do not stay on the line if it would be dangerous or make noise that may give away your location to the shooter.
- Efforts will be made to alert the building of the active-shooter situation. However, there may be times when broadcasting over the radio system is not feasible. Staff should not wait for a formal announcement to take action.

- If an announcement can be made, it is vital that we use plain language and call this an active-shooter situation. Do not use code words, as they can create confusion.
- Staff should attempt to remain calm and keep the children in their care calm and quiet.
- **Hide, flee, or fight:** If you are able to hide, you should lock and barricade your doors, turn off the lights, hide the children, and stay quiet. The goal is to make the room/area look unoccupied.
- If there is no possibility of escaping or hiding, when your life is in imminent danger, you should make a personal choice to protect yourself and the children in your care. This includes distracting, overpowering, and disabling the shooter, if possible.
- If you are able to evacuate, run with the children until you are far away from the facility. Stay low and use items for concealment as you are making your escape.
- Do not pull the fire alarm.
- Once you have reached a safe distance, be sure you keep the children together. Conduct a head count and identify any missing children from your classroom.
- Stay far away from the facility until contacted by the director or instructed by law enforcement.
- Staff should not make statements to the media or families unless instructed to do so to prevent rumors or misinformation. If asked, respond, "We are following our emergency procedures," and direct them to the site spokesperson.
- **When law enforcement arrives:** Remain calm, and follow officers' instructions.
- Put down any items in your hands, such as bags or jackets. Immediately raise your hands and spread your fingers. Keep your hands visible.
- Avoid making quick movements toward officers such as attempting to hold on to them for safety.
- It is likely that law enforcement will ask for your help with reuniting families with children. Be prepared to provide law enforcement with information related to the children in your classroom and care.

Policy on Sheltering in Place

Purpose: Sheltering in place is used for a wide variety of emergencies, such as during severe weather such as tornadoes; during some environmental hazards such as earthquakes, dangerous smoke from a wildfire, chemical contamination, or radiation incidents; or during local emergencies such as short-duration utility outages. Going outside or trying to evacuate in these situations would put personal health and safety at risk; therefore, staying put is the best option.

Procedure: Provide physical separation from something hazardous in the outdoor environment. Shelter-in-place situations can take various forms. For some of the more severe threats, it will be important to move children and staff into the center of the building. Put as many solid walls between you and the threat as possible. For shelter-in-place situations that are less severe, students and staff may be more comfortable remaining in their normal classrooms.

Chain of Command

The director or business manager shall determine whether a lockdown is needed.

Once a shelter-in-place order has been given, the director shall assume command and control of the situation. If the director is unavailable, then the business manager shall assume the duties assigned to the director. If both the director and business manager are unavailable, then the lead teacher with the most seniority shall assume command and control.

Responsibilities of the Person in Charge

1. Ensure staff is advised of the situation and the potential hazard.
2. If this is a severe-weather event, assign one person to listen the NOAA weather radio or the local FM emergency channels.
3. Once the situation is deemed over or stabilized, determine whether early dismissal is appropriate or if it is safe to return to normal programming at the facility.
4. Determine the appropriate communication strategy. This may require communicating with families, licensing, and community officials.
5. During a shelter-in-place event, individuals will not be allowed in or out of the program areas. Doors will remain closed and locked. Keep this in mind when communicating with families, as they will not be allowed to retrieve their children. Further, severe weather may prevent families from reaching our location. If communicating with families, it will be important to have them remain where they are until the shelter-in-place event is over.

Responsibilities of Staff

1. Keep calm and take measures so as not to frighten the children.
2. Depending on the emergency, you may be instructed to move away from windows and into an interior area of the building, or you may be asked to stay in your room. The nature of the emergency will dictate the response.
3. Keep children safe and calm until the shelter-in-place event is over. Attempt to make this a normal day by engaging them in quiet games or softly reading books to them.

Policy on Family Reunification

Purpose: This plan describes the reunification process that we will use in the event that parents/guardians need to pick up their children after an emergency or disaster has occurred. Our goal is to provide a process that ensures the safe, orderly, and documented reunion of children with their parents/guardians.

Procedure: Upon enrollment in our program, families will be provided with information related to our reunification procedure. Families will be asked to fill out a form that details the contact information for the family, as well as a list of individuals authorized to pick up the child. We will discuss with the families our normal pickup procedure and how our procedure in an emergency or disaster may differ. As emergency contact information can change, we ask that families notify us of any changes in contact information or in authorized individuals. Twice a year, we will also ask families to update this information.

The Family Reunification Plan will be activated by the director or her designee. The activation should occur as soon as possible after an incident occurs that warrants reunification. The safety of staff and children is paramount, and those efforts designed to save and protect life take priority. Once the director or designee decides to activate the plan, staff members should be notified in person or by walkie-talkie or cell phone.

Reunification Process

During an emergency or disaster, stress levels will be high. It is easy to get overwhelmed while responding to many different competing demands. Further, reunification may occur off-site in an environment that is unfamiliar. Therefore, staff should maintain control, order, and accountability of all children. This process is designed to enhance accountability by creating a record and authentication process before the release of each child.

- **Step 1: Establish a parent/guardian check-in.** Families will check in when they first arrive at the reunification location. They will complete a student information card and provide appropriate identification so that reunification team members may verify their identities. Parents or guardians should be informed that the reunification process is intended to protect both the safety of the child and provide for an accountable transfer of the child from the custody of the school to a recognized custodial parent or guardian.
- **Step 2: Establish child waiting area.** Children will be asked to wait in a separate area until a parent or guardian arrives to pick them up. Children will be engaged by staff in ways that minimize the exposure to the emergency or disaster and imitate a normal day as much as possible. It is not advisable to have families go directly to the child waiting area, as the reunification of families may cause other children anxiety, fear, or grief.
- **Step 3: Establish a parent/guardian waiting area.** Once families have checked in and identification has been verified, families will be asked to wait in an area while their child is retrieved. A staff member will communicate to

the child waiting area via walkie-talkie, runner, or phone, and the child will be brought to the family.

Sample of Checklist to Maintain Accountability of Family Reunification

Child's Name	Assigned Classroom	Parent/Guardian Name	ID Provided?	Time Child Released

References and Recommended Reading

Bethell, Christina, et al. 2019. "Positive Childhood Experiences and Adult Mental and Relational Health in a Statewide Sample: Associations across Adverse Childhood Experiences Levels." *Journal of the American Medical Association* 173(11): e193007. https://jamanetwork.com/journals/jamapediatrics/fullarticle/2749336

Campbell, Richard. 2017. *Structure Fires in Educational Properties*. Quincy, MA: National Fire Protection Association.

Caron, Christina. 2017. "84 Percent of Puerto Rico Still Doesn't Have Power." *The New York Times*, October 10. https://www.nytimes.com/2017/10/10/us/puerto-rico-recovery.html

CBS News. 2012. "Sandy Takes Out 25 Percent of Cell Towers." CBSNews.com. https://www.cbsnews.com/news/sandy-takes-out-25-percent-of-cell-towers/

Centers for Disease Control and Prevention. 2012. "Lesson 1: Introduction to Epidemiology. Section 11: Epidemic Disease Occurrence." *In Principles of Epidemiology in Public Health Practice: An Introduction to Applied Epidemiology and Biostatistics.* 3rd ed. Atlanta: Centers for Disease Control and Prevention. https://www.cdc.gov/csels/dsepd/ss1978/lesson1/section11.html

Centers for Disease Control and Prevention. 2019a. "Community NPIs: Flu Prevention in Community Settings." Nonpharmaceutical Interventions (NPIs). https://www.cdc.gov/nonpharmaceutical-interventions/community/index.html

Centers for Disease Control and Prevention. 2019b. "Preventing Adverse Childhood Experiences." Violence Prevention. https://www.cdc.gov/violenceprevention/childabuseandneglect/aces/fastfact.html?CDC_AA_refVal=https%3A%2F%2Fwww.cdcgov%2Fviolenceprevention%2Fchildabuseandneglect%2Facestudy%2Faboutace.html

Centers for Disease Control and Prevention. 2020. "Vaccine Effectiveness: How Well Do the Flu Vaccines Work?" Influenza (Flu). https://www.cdc.gov/flu/vaccines-work/vaccineeffect.htm

Child Care and Development Block Grant Act of 2014. 42 U.S.C. § 9858c(c)(2)(U).

Child Care and Development Fund. 2019. Plan Provisions. 45 CFR 98.45(I)(2)(i).

Community Partnership of the Ozarks. n.d. *Don't Let One Disaster Lead to Another: Disaster Toolkit*. Springfield, MO: Community Partnership of the Ozarks. https://mema.maryland.gov/Documents/Local%20Recovery%20Planning%20Support%20Toolkit/Long%20Term%20Recovery%20Committee%20Guide%20and%20Resources/Case%20Studies/Joplin,%20MO%20Case%20Study%20Information%20

and%20Materials/Responding%20to%20a%20Disaster%20A%20
Prevention%20Toolkit%20(Joplin).pdf

Committee for Economic Development. 2019. *Child Care in State Economies: 2019 Update*. Arlington, VA: Committee for Economic Development of The Conference Board.

Delamater, Paul, et al. 2019. "Complexity of the Basic Reproduction Number (R0)." *Emerging Infectious Diseases* 25(1): 1–4.

Doherty, Aine. 2014. "SMS versus Email Marketing." Business 2 Economy. https://www.business2community.com/digital-marketing/sms-versus-email-marketing-0957139#!bth7SG

Dudley, William. 2020. "An Assessment of the 2019 Mobile Industry Predictions." *D!gitalist Magazine*, January 13. https://www.digitalistmag.com/digital-economy/2020/01/13/assessment-of-2019-mobile-industry-predictions-06202240/

Eschner, Kat. 2019. "The Most Dangerous Places to Live in America that Are Prone to Natural Disasters." CNBC. https://www.cnbc.com/2019/07/10/billion-dollar-natural-disasters-rising-these-states-better-prepare.html

Express Scripts. 2020. "America's State of Mind Report." Express Scripts. https://www.express-scripts.com/corporate/americas-state-of-mind-report?mod=article_inline

Federal Communications Commission. n.d. "Wireless 911 Service." Federal Communications Commission. https://www.fcc.gov/consumers/guides/911-wireless-services

Federal Emergency Management Agency. n.d.a. *Make Your Business Resilient.* Washington, DC: US Department of Homeland Security. https://www.fema.gov/media-library-data/1441212988001-1aa7fa978c5f999ed088dcaa815cb8cd/3a_BusinessInfographic-1.pdf

Federal Emergency Management Agency. n.d.b. *Ready Business Power Outage Toolkit*. Washington, DC: US Department of Homeland Security. https://www.fema.gov/media-library-data/1510690314175-1e6c4874b251c3022ac4b57b0369e2da/Power_Outage_Ready_Business_Toolkit_Interactive_Final_508.pdf

Federal Emergency Management Agency. n.d.c. *Ready Business Quakesmart Toolkit*. Washington, DC: US Department of Homeland Security. https://www.fema.gov/media-library-data/1510690321803-1e6c4874b251c3022ac4b57b0369e2da/QuakeSmart_Ready_Business_Toolkit_Interactive_Final_508.pdf

Federal Emergency Management Agency. 2010. *FEMA Disaster Assistance Fact Sheet: Public Assistance for Child Care Services.* Washington, DC: US

Department of Health and Human Services. https://www.acf.hhs.gov/sites/
    default/files/occ/fema_public_assistance_for_child_care_services.pdf

Federal Emergency Management Agency. 2011. *National Disaster Recovery
    Framework: Strengthening Disaster Recovery for the Nation.* Washington,
    DC: US Department of Homeland Security. https://www.fema.gov/pdf/
    recoveryframework/ndrf.pdf

Federal Emergency Management Agency. 2013. "IS-111.A.: Livestock in
    Disasters." In *Emergency Management in the United States: Unit 4.*
    Emmitsburg, MD: Emergency Management Institute. https://training.fema.
    gov/emiweb/downloads/is111_unit%204.pdf

Federal Emergency Management Agency. 2016. "Crisis Communication Plan."
    Ready.gov. https://www.ready.gov/business/implementation/crisis

Federal Emergency Management Agency. 2018. "Federal Insurance and Mitigation
    Administration." US Department of Homeland Security. https://www.fema.gov/
    what-mitigation/federal-insurance-mitigation-administration#

Federal Emergency Management Agency. 2019. "Disaster Declarations by Year."
    US Department of Homeland Security. https://www.fema.gov/disasters/
    year/2019?field_dv2_declaration_type_value=All

Federal Emergency Management Agency. 2020a. "Community Emergency
    Response Team." Ready.gov. https://www.ready.gov/cert

Federal Emergency Management Agency. 2020b. "Emergency Alerts." Ready.gov.
    https://www.ready.gov/alerts

Foodsafety.gov. 2019. "Food Safety in a Disaster or Emergency." Foodsafety.
    gov. https://www.foodsafety.gov/keep-food-safe/food-safety-in-disaster-or-
    emergency

Glynn, Sarah Jane, and Danielle Corley. 2016. "The Cost of Work-Family Policy
    Inaction." Center for American Progress. https://www.americanprogress.org/
    issues/women/reports/2016/09/22/143877/the-cost-of-inaction/

Government of Canada. 2015. "Staying in Touch during Emergencies." Get
    Prepared. https://www.getprepared.gc.ca/cnt/plns/styngtchmrgncs-en.aspx

Guynn, Jessica. 2020. "Coronavirus Child Care Crisis Tops Concerns as Nation
    Pushes to Reopen. Parents Ask: Who Will Watch Our Children?" USA Today,
    May 17. https://www.usatoday.com/story/money/2020/05/17/coronavirus-
    childcare-america-reopening-trump-fauci/5194811002/

Healthline Media. 2020. "What to Know about Viruses." *Medical News
    Today.* Healthline Media UK Ltd. https://www.medicalnewstoday.com/
    articles/158179#transmission

Institute for Childhood Preparedness. 2019a. "Georgia Hosts Child Care Provider Preparedness Workshop." Institute for Childhood Preparedness. https://www.childhoodpreparedness.org/post/wrap-up-georgia

Institute for Childhood Preparedness. 2019b. "Revisiting the 2014 Winter Ice Storm 'Snow Jam' in Atlanta, Georgia." Institute for Childhood Preparedness. https://www.childhoodpreparedness.org/post/revisiting-the-2014-winter-ice-storm-in-atlanta-georgia

Leitl, Eugen. 2006. "Information Technology Issues during and after Katrina and Usefulness of the Internet: How We Mobilized and Utilized Digital Communications Systems." *Critical Care* 10(1): 110.

Leser, Kendall A., Julie Looper-Coats, and Andrew R. Roszak. 2019. "Emergency Preparedness Plans and Perceptions among a Sample of United States Childcare Providers." *Journal of Disaster Medicine and Public Health Preparedness* 13(4): 704–708.

Murrin, Suzanne. 2015. *The Response to Superstorm Sandy Highlights the Importance of Recovery Planning for Child Care Nationwide*. Washington, DC: US Department of Health and Human Services, Office of the Inspector General. https://oig.hhs.gov/oei/reports/oei-04-14-00410.pdf

National Center for Education Statistics. 2019. "Fast Facts." National Center for Education Statistics. https://nces.ed.gov/fastfacts/display.asp?id=372

National Disaster Education Coalition. 1999. "Why Talk About Tornadoes?" Disaster Center. http://www.disastercenter.com/guide/tornado.html

National Oceanic and Atmospheric Administration. 2019. "What Is Storm Surge?" National Ocean Service. https://oceanservice.noaa.gov/facts/stormsurge-stormtide.html

National Oceanic and Atmospheric Administration, National Centers for Environmental Information. 2020. "U.S. Billion-Dollar Weather and Climate Disasters." National Oceanic and Atmospheric Administration. https://www.ncdc.noaa.gov/billions/

National Resource Center for Health and Safety in Child Care and Early Education. 2020. "Caring for Our Children." National Resource Center for Health and Safety in Child Care and Early Education. https://nrckids.org/CFOC/Database/7

National Severe Storms Laboratory. n.d. "Severe Weather 101—Tornadoes." National Severe Storms Laboratory, National Oceanic and Atmospheric Administration. https://www.nssl.noaa.gov/education/svrwx101/tornadoes/

National Weather Service. n.d.a. "Hurricane Facts." National Weather Service, National Oceanic and Atmospheric Administration. https://www.weather.gov/

source/zhu/ZHU_Training_Page/tropical_stuff/hurricane_anatomy/hurricane_
anatomy.html

National Weather Service. n.d.b. "NOAA Weather Radio Frequently Asked
Questions." National Weather Service, National Oceanic and Atmospheric
Administration. https://www.weather.gov/phi/nwrfaq

National Weather Service. n.d.c. "Thunderstorm Hazards—Tornadoes." National
Weather Service, National Oceanic and Atmospheric Administration. https://
www.weather.gov/jetstream/tornado

National Weather Service. n.d.d. "Turn Around Don't Drown." National Weather
Service, National Oceanic and Atmospheric Administration. https://www.
weather.gov/safety/flood-turn-around-dont-drown

Office of Child Care. 2017. *Statewide Disaster Plan (or Disaster Plan for a Tribe's
Service Area) for Child Care*. Washington, DC: US Department of Health and
Human Services, Administration for Children and Families.

Office of Disease Prevention and Health Promotion. 2020. "Appendix 14. Food
Safety Principles and Guidance." In *Dietary Guidelines 2015–2020*. Washington,
DC: US Department of Health and Human Services. https://health.gov/our-
work/food-nutrition/2015-2020-dietary-guidelines/guidelines/appendix-14/

Office of Head Start. 2018a. "1302.47 Safety Practices." Head Start Early
Childhood Learning and Knowledge Center. https://eclkc.ohs.acf.hhs.gov/
policy/45-cfr-chap-xiii/1302-47-safety-practices

Office of Head Start. 2018b. "Fiscal Year 2019 Head Start Funding Increase."
Head Start Early Childhood Learning and Knowledge Center. https://eclkc.ohs.
acf.hhs.gov/policy/pi/acf-pi-hs-18-06

Office of Head Start. 2018c. *Head Start Program Facts: Fiscal Year 2018*.
Washington, DC: US Department of Health and Human Services,
Administration for Children and Families, Head Start Early Childhood Learning
and Knowledge Center. https://eclkc.ohs.acf.hhs.gov/sites/default/files/pdf/
no-search/hs-program-fact-sheet-2018.pdf

Olensky, Steve. 2013. "Pulling Back the Curtain on Text Message
Mobile Marketing." *Forbes*, March 4. https://www.forbes.com/sites/
marketshare/2013/03/04/pulling-back-the-curtain-on-text-message-mobile-
marketing/#446b458c10d9

OnSolve. 2020. "Handle Critical Events with CodeRED Mass Notification." OnSolve.
https://www.onsolve.com/solutions/products/codered/

Petkova, Elisaveta, et al. 2016. *The American Preparedness Project: Where
the US Public Stands in 2015*. Research Brief 2016_2. New York: National

Center for Disaster Preparedness, Earth Institute, Columbia University. https://academiccommons.columbia.edu/doi/10.7916/D84Q7TZN

Public Health Emergency. 2020. "Medical Reserve Corps." US Department of Health and Human Services. https://www.phe.gov/about/oem/prep/Pages/mrc.aspx

Quadir, Regina. 2012. "Startling Facts You Should Know about Disaster Preparedness." Blog. Centers for Disease Control and Prevention. https://blogs.cdc.gov/publichealthmatters/2012/07/startling-facts-you-should-know-about-disaster-preparedness/

Region II Head Start Association. 2019. "Update: Puerto Rico Disaster Recovery." Region II Head Start Association. http://www.region2headstart.org/post/puerto-rico-disaster-recovery

Roszak, Andrew R. 2017. "Child's Play: Remembering Our Youngest in Disaster Planning." *IAEM Bulletin* 2017(7): 29–30. https://www.iaem.org/portals/25/documents/Andrew-Roszak-Article-July2017-IAEM-Bulletin.pdf

Roszak, Andrew R. 2019. "Using STREAM Techniques after Disasters to Keep Kids Learning and Engaged." FunShine Blog. https://funshineblog.com/2019/10/18/using-stream-techniques-after-disasters-to-keep-kids-learning-and-engaged/

Santa Clara County Public Health Department. n.d. "Information about Social Distancing." Fact Sheet. https://www.cidrap.umn.edu/sites/default/files/public/php/185/185_factsheet_social_distancing.pdf

Save the Children. 2015. *Still at Risk: U. S. Children 10 Years After Hurricane Katrina*. Fairfield, CT: Save the Children. https://rems.ed.gov/docs/DisasterReport_2015.pdf

Schaefer, Stephanie, Susan L. Gates, and Mike Kiernan. 2013. *Strengthening Missouri Businesses through Investments in Early Care and Education.* Washington, DC: America's Edge. https://dss.mo.gov/cbec/pdf/americas-edge-report-2013.pdf

Schlegelmilch, Jeff. 2018. "Disaster Preparedness: Resilient Children Are Vital." *Disaster Relief and Recovery Magazine*, July 12, https://givingcompass.org/disaster-relief-recovery/disaster-preparedness-resilient-children-are-vital/

Seattle Office of Emergency Management. n.d. *Family Reunification: Emergency Procedures for Families and Students*. Seattle, WA: Seattle Office of Emergency Management. https://www.seattle.gov/Documents/Departments/Emergency/Preparedness/Family%20Reunification/2017-05-26%20OUTREACH.%20Schools.%20Family%20Reunification%20Training.pdf

Sesame Street in Communities. n.d. "Handling Emergencies." Sesame Street in Communities. https://sesamestreetincommunities.org/topics/emergency-preparedness/

Smith, Adam B. 2019. "2018's Billion Dollar Disasters in Context." NOAA Climate. gov. https://www.climate.gov/news-features/blogs/beyond-data/2018s-billion-dollar-disasters-context

Stevens, Katharine B. 2017. *Workforce of Today, Workforce of Tomorrow: The Business Case for High-Quality Childcare*. Washington, DC: US Chamber of Commerce Foundation. https://www.uschamberfoundation.org/sites/default/files/Workforce%20of%20Today%20Workforce%20of%20Tomorrow%20Report.pdf

Storm Prediction Center. 2020. "Enhanced F Scale for Tornado Damage." Storm Prediction Center, National Oceanic and Atmospheric Administration. https://www.spc.noaa.gov/faq/tornado/ef-scale.html

Sullivan, Laura, and Emma Schwartz. 2018. "FEMA Report Acknowledges Failures in Puerto Rico Disaster Response." NPR. https://www.npr.org/2018/07/13/628861808/fema-report-acknowledges-failures-in-puerto-rico-disaster-response

Total Security Solutions. 2018. "Using Big Data to Prevent and Mitigate School Shootings." Blog. Total Security Solutions. https://www.tssbulletproof.com/blog/big-data-prevent-school-shootings/

University of Rhode Island. 2015. "Glossary." Hurricanes: Science and Society. http://www.hurricanescience.org/glossary/?letter=E#glossaryword354

US Department of Labor, Bureau of Labor Statistics. 2020. "Employment Characteristics of Families—2019." US Department of Labor, Bureau of Labor Statistics. https://www.bls.gov/news.release/pdf/famee.pdf

US Department of Transportation. 2018. "Nine Classes of Hazardous Materials." Federal Motor Carrier Safety Administration. https://www.fmcsa.dot.gov/sites/fmcsa.dot.gov/files/docs/Nine_Classes_of_Hazardous_Materials-4-2013_508CLN.pdf

US Environmental Protection Agency. 2019a. "EPA Map of Radon Zones." US Environmental Protection Agency. https://www.epa.gov/radon/epa-map-radon-zones

US Environmental Protection Agency. 2019b. "Local Emergency Planning Committees." US Environmental Protection Agency. https://www.epa.gov/epcra/local-emergency-planning-committees

US Marine Corps. n.d. "Ready Marine Corps: Emergency Preparedness Program." Marines. https://www.ready.marines.mil/Make-a-Plan/Making-a-Family-Emergency-Plan/

US Nuclear Regulatory Commission. 2018. "Emergency Planning Zones." US Nuclear Regulatory Commission. https://www.nrc.gov/about-nrc/emerg-preparedness/about-emerg-preparedness/planning-zones.html

Whitebook, Marcy, et al. 2018. *Early Childhood Workforce Index 2018.* Berkeley, CA: Center for the Study of Child Care Employment, University of California, Berkeley. https://cscce.berkeley.edu/files/2018/06/Early-Childhood-Workforce-Index-2018.pdf

World Health Organization. 2005. *Violence and Disasters.* Geneva, Switzerland: World Health Organization. https://www.who.int/violence_injury_prevention/publications/violence/violence_disasters.pdf

Index

Sheltering in place, 9, 36–37
    chain of command, 71
    policy on, 70–71
    procedure, 70–71
    purpose of policy, 70
    responsibilities of person in charge, 71
    responsibilities of staff, 71
Smith, Adam B., 7
Smoke detectors, 8
Snacks, 38, 50, 54
Social distancing
    defined, 32
Social media, 24, 28
Staff turnover, 22, 27, 57
Stevens, Katharine B., 1, 11
Storm Prediction Center, 50
Storm surge
    defined, 47
STREAM education, 60
Substance abuse
    ACES and, 12–13
    after disasters, 12–13
Suicides
    after disasters, 13
Sullivan, Laura, 24
Sump pumps, 44
Superstorm Sandy, 3
    communication outages, 24
Surge protectors, 55
    defined, 54

T
Tabletop exercises, 59
Telephone calling trees, 24
Terrorist attacks
    Oklahoma City bombing, 12
    September 11, 12
Testing/revising your emergency plan,
    57–60
    importance of exercises, 58
    required drills, 58
    tabletop and cognitive exercises, 59
Texting, 24, 28
    alerts, 19
    vs. emailing, 27
Thermal harm
    defined, 52
Threat and Hazard Identification and Risk
    Assessments, 17–18
Tornado warning
    defined, 49
Tornado watch
    defined, 49
Tornadoes, 49–51
    community risk assessment, 17–18
    perceived preparedness for, 10

    lingo, 49–50
    considerations for child care, 50–51
    Joplin, Mo., 12–13
Total Security Solutions, 18
Training on responding, 20–21
Transparency, 25
Transportation for evacuation, 39
Trauma
    child care's role in mitigating, 12–13
Tsunamis
    evacuation, 37
Turn Around, Don't Drown! 44–45
Twitter, 24

U
Unity of messaging, 23, 25
Universal procedures, 33
University of Rhode Island, 47
US Department of Health and Human
    Services, 2
US Department of Homeland Security, 25
US Department of Labor
    Bureau of Labor Statistics, 2
US Department of Transportation
    Emergency Response Guidebook, 53
    Hazard Classification System, 52
US Economic Census 2012, 11
US Environmental Protection Agency, 18
US Geological Survey, 17
US Marine Corps, 29
US Nuclear Regulatory Commission, 17

V
Vaccination, 31, 34
Violence. See Active shooter events;
    Domestic violence
Viruses, 34–35
    COVID-19, 3, 12
    defined, 32
    RNA-based, 34
Volcanoes
    community risk assessment, 17–18
Vulnerable populations, 16–17

W
Water, 36, 38, 50, 54
Weather Channel app, 26
Weather disasters
    costs rising, 7
"What if?" work, 25
Whitebook, Marcy, 1
Wild fires
    evacuation, 37
    sheltering in place, 36
Wireless Emergency Alerts, 25
Working mothers, 2
World Health Organization, 12